CORO-CORO

Coro-coro, the Scarlet Ibis.

CORO-CORO

*The World of the
Scarlet Ibis*

by Paul A. Zahl

Foreword
by Joseph Wood Krutch

THE BOBBS-MERRILL COMPANY, INC.
Publishers
Indianapolis   New York

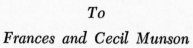

To
Frances and Cecil Munson

By Way of Acknowledgment:

In 1949, in response to an inquiry, Dr. Robert Cushman Murphy of the American Museum of Natural History referred me to the Phelps family of Caracas. It was the distinguished head of that family, Dr. William H. Phelps, together with his son, William H. Phelps, Jr., who directed me to Venezuela's inland State of Apure. There I met and mingled for a time with a small multitude of kind and good people who inhabit those seasonally flooded and biologically teeming llanos plains. Finally I found that for which I had come—and more.

Early associated with these circumstances were Dr. John Oliver La Gorce, president of the National Geographic Society, and the Society's Research Committee, without whose strong confidence the search herein described would not have been undertaken.

I am much pleased, as the author of any book relating to natural history would surely be, to name these whose reading of the manuscript wholly or in part was invaluable: Dr. William Beebe of the New York Zoological Society, D. Dwight Davis of the Chicago Museum of Natural History, Dr. Robert Cushman Murphy and Dr. Charles M. Breder, Jr., both of the American Museum of Natural History, Dr. Caryl P. Haskins of the Haskins Laboratories, and William H. Phelps, Jr. I wish to express thanks to Venezuelan ranchmen John P. Kitson and H. L. E. Briggs, not only for their having verified narrative details in the manuscript but for all earlier kindnesses. For valued editorial guidance I am indebted to Hiram Haydn and Elizabeth Bragdon of The Bobbs-Merrill Company.

Finally, had not Eda Zahl, my wife, collaborated in every aspect of the planning and preparation of this book, I doubt if there would have been a book.

Grateful acknowledgment is made of the permission given by the National Geographic Society to reproduce certain map and picture material. Opinions and attitudes expressed in this book are, of course, those of the author and are not necessarily to be considered as shared by the persons or institutions mentioned above.

PAUL A. ZAHL

List of Illustrations

Coro-coro, the Scarlet Ibis — *Frontispiece*

Map of the State of Apure — *Facing page 18*

The swollen Río Apure threatens San Fernando

Two cement ribbons pave most streets in San Fernando

"Coro-coros?"

Wooden dugouts, the chief means of winter transportation

The wharf at San Fernando

The sullen character of the rainy season reflects in faces seen

The Río Apure at crest

Disembarcation in the tall grass

Three river companions

Between pages 48-49

The caribe of Venezuela

Waterbirds—but no coro-coros

A crocodile at the riverbank

Anhinga nests

Llanos friends

A llanos lizard

Cattle along the riverbank

Hoofed pork going to market

The doctor's nurse

Between pages 112-113

Setting out in Kitson's 22-horse-powered dugout

The author and his aides at Algarrobito

A peon family and assorted guests

Ducks for the table

Kitson amuses himself with a snake

Mealtime in a llanos hut

The author repairs his monkscloth birdblind

A world of trailing lianas

Between pages 150-151

LIST OF ILLUSTRATIONS—*Continued*

Portrait of a Scarlet Ibis
Scarlet Ibis in flight
A parent arrives to feed its young
This young ibis has not yet learned to fly
The author, his outboard and a scarlet captive
The author entering his birdblind
The 20-foot long dugout spurts ahead
Its blunt beak and unsharpened toenails provide
    few weapons for the Scarlet Ibis
The beauty of the Scarlet Ibis
Wingtips and nest clutch of the Scarlet Ibis
The hoatzin
The boat-billed night heron
A maguari stork

Between pages 208-209

Foreword:

South America is nowadays the real Dark Continent. Few parts of Africa are still so isolated, so inaccessible, so dangerous or so little known as much of the vast area in the drainage basins of the great South American rivers. Partly because of the heat, the humidity and the almost unchecked prevalence of tropical diseases, white civilization has changed this country little. The few from outside who settle there are more likely to "go native" than to change the natives' own way of life.

Not surprisingly, this country has also been the subject of some of the gaudiest and least convincing traveler's tales told in recent times. Even the now half-legendary Colonel Fawcett, who was a genius in his own way and told the truth as he saw it, was possessed by extravagant notions. Others less competent and probably less honest have demonstrably pulled either the reader's leg or, perhaps, their own with all-too-colorful tales of high adventure suspiciously centered around the more accessible portions of the region they pretend to have explored.

Fortunately the present narrative is a different matter, and perhaps the first of its virtues is that it is obviously unvarnished. Dr. Zahl got deep into pretty remote country. He saw some strange sights and ran into some serious dangers. But he never strives too hard to impress and he never overcolors what is colorful enough. Not a professional adventurer but a laboratory biologist engaged in cancer research, he has the training to understand the meaning of what he sees and a temperament that puts respect for accuracy before any desire to impress. Posing as no superman in daring or endurance, he sometimes encourages the reader in the delusion that he could almost do the same himself.

The very fact that his quest was a limited and rather

minor one has its advantage. Instead of setting out like some of his predecessors to discover lost cities, hidden treasures, prehistoric animals or the survivors from Atlantis, he merely wanted to find the breeding grounds of the scarlet ibis and to see whether this bird—a rather drab pink in the few zoo collections where it is to be found—really was the flame-colored jewel described long ago by the only previous travelers who seem to have seen it in its native haunt. This, as it turned out, was quite enough for one expedition.

As usual in such matters, everybody professed to be familiar with the bird in question but had usually seen it somewhere else, or at some other season, or during some other year. If, for a change, the informant claimed to know where it was at the moment, then he had always to admit after some long, perilous journey up swollen rivers or through trackless flood plains that for some reason or other it didn't happen to be there now.

Finally persistence won; the birds were as colorful as they were supposed to be; and readers of the *National Geographic* will remember the fine series of photographs Dr. Zahl was able to take. In this book he describes the whole adventure and its two climaxes: one when, after so many disappointments, the birds were actually there; the other after the birds were found but when he himself was lost— in the company of a guide just as lost as he was.

Dr. Zahl is a thoughtful man as well as a technically trained one, and there are those who will find his biologist's comments on what he saw and the speculative thoughts which often intruded into his scientific mind at least as interesting as the adventure itself. In that part of nearly equatorial Venezuela nature furnished what seemed to be, at least for plant life, almost optimum conditions. During the whole winter the temperature never varies, day or night, outside the 80-85-degree range, the humidity is almost 100 per cent, and the sunlight is diffused both by prevalent clouds and by the green canopy of the higher-growing plants. The steady warmth, the moisture and the softened sunlight produce an almost incredibly green green. The waterway which Dr. Zahl threaded in a dugout powered by an outboard motor is closed in by green walls on both sides, and in the daytime the silence is so complete that the walls seem to enclose an empty land. Yet "I knew that behind the leafy façades to the right and left monkeys sat, tree frogs clung, snakes coiled, lizards ran, birds perched and insects crawled—dozens of some, millions of others, all, during the daylight hours, quietly molten into their chosen backgrounds."

Yet all this was very far from being a Paradise-before-the-Fall. Notoriously, it is in the hot, moist regions that nature's ways seem hardest to reconcile with man's needs, either material or spiritual. Malignant diseases flourish so abundantly that to be ill rather than to be well is the "normal" condition of the human inhabitants. Vines and grasses as well as trees make impenetrable jungles or swallow up men's clearings. Some of the most gorgeously beautiful as well as some of the most loathsome forms of life flourish there side by side. Before Dr. Zahl saw his flame-colored birds he saw also toads which could not escape and possibly did not want to escape from the privy pit in which they had probably been confined for years.

Such animals as the jaguar, the crocodile and the caribe —the savage little fish which will strip the flesh from a man's bones in a few minutes—suggest ancient savageries almost forgotten in temperate regions. The lives of most creatures here are unusually violent and unusually short. Birth, maturation, death and decay are all speeded up. The competitive struggle for existence, "the survival of the fittest" (but fittest for what?), may be more naked and brutal here than elsewhere, and the very headlong exuberance of life appears somehow indecent. In no other region does "Nature's kindly law" become a phrase so obviously satiric. Where does man, with desires and standards seemingly so different, fit in? Or doesn't he fit in at all? Is he a child of nature or a rebel against her? Should he try to accord himself with her or war against her?

As a research scientist normally sustained by the hope that at some distant day what he discovers may contribute to the saving of lives that cancer would otherwise have ended, Dr. Zahl is in a position that makes such questions inevitable, and it is obvious that they interested him at least as much as the nesting habits of the scarlet ibis. Is man inexorably bound by the law of the jungle and is the whole of that law no more than what appears on the surface of jungle life? Why should anyone be concerned with the possibility of preventing cancer some years hence?

Being a scientist by profession, Dr. Zahl is very reluctant to toy with any answers which science itself does not support. Yet also is he aware that all the answers which the standard methods of orthodox science have been able to give are unsatisfying. "Is the human individual, like all biological creatures, a perennially expendable entity, with no significance beyond that which a single organism has always had as one of the pawns of evolution? As a biologist, I had no basis for any other than an affirmative answer. As all too human a being, I found such an answer violently unsatisfactory."

But is there anywhere except in the realm of science to ask these questions? "Some sense, some profess to know, that man is more than a mere gene carrier for his species; but who can prove it, who can articulate it? Our physiologists, psychologists and psychiatrists have done so thorough a job that a prophet, keeping within the context of modern science, who can demonstrate that the human individual is something more than a biochemical system reacting to its environment might well find the world at mid-twentieth century a fertile field."

Deep in the llanos country—like the Everglades in winter, like the Pampas in summer—Dr. Zahl came across a youngish German physician who had renounced civiliza-

tion after the war and was now charged by the Venezuelan government with improving the health of the natives. He had a kerosene refrigerator reasonably well stocked with modern drugs and biologicals. Sick natives came and were usually dewormed. Then they carried "wonder drugs" away with them, but when no miracle had occurred within a few days they were likely to toss the medicines away. The two medical men discussed the situation and trod warily around the edges of the great philosophical questions. But apparently Dr. Zahl never asked what he would no doubt have liked to ask: Now that the German doctor had seen both, what did he think of the comparative merits of what he had got away from and what he had got into?

An ancient joke explained the failure of a certain Roman citizen to profit from travel by the fact that "he took himself along for company." It is obvious that in the present case Dr. Zahl could not have had better. What he brought along was at least as interesting as what he found.

JOSEPH WOOD KRUTCH

Chapter 1

THE PLANE had been scheduled to leave the Maiquetía airfield at eight in the morning. In best mañana tradition, we left at ten. Up, up, like a spiraling buzzard, until the 9,000-foot coastal range no longer towered; then due south through a pass between two dry scrub-covered peaks close on either side. Latin American pilots are said to be among the best in the world, but the knowledge was of no outstanding comfort to me. Abruptly we burst through the range and out over a vastness of rolling brown foothills.

In Spanish I directed a labored sentence of inquiry, first at the hostess, then at the heavy man on the seat next to me who had tucked a great napkin under his chin preparatory to digging into a lunch basket the size of his lap. Each looked back at me with a blank face and made apologetic shrugs. My smattering of book Spanish conveyed no meaning.

A small boy ventured down the aisle, and stopped and studied me. He said something in a loud voice that must have been very bad, for the other eight or ten passengers, including his mother several seats ahead, quickly turned to look. For a moment the motor noise was masked by the mother's rapid, streaming, scolding Spanish; the boy retreated obediently, but continued to stare. I could say nothing; my ears did not translate, and my tongue was

17

caught in the pages of that little dictionary bulging my shirt pocket.

At Macuto and Caracas I had been unaware of the language matter, for there almost everyone I met spoke perfect English. But here now in this llanos-bound DC-3, amid a load of provincially tongued Venezuelans, I felt dumb and solitary. It was a terrible punishment that God inflicted on the builders of Babel.

The brown foothills and rolling country were gradually giving way to a perfect flatness, empty to the horizon. I thought of Columbus and appreciated the character qualities that had led him to sail into the mysterious void of the western Atlantic. Indicating perhaps my own lack of Columbian fiber, I slumped in my air-borne seat and yielded to a feeling of inquietude. The strange faces, the unintelligible language, the uncertainty of what lay ahead at my destination—these canceled that buoyancy which, on the basis of previous travel experience, the unfolding wonders of the earth's surface should have engendered in me. The glamour of my romance with the scarlet ibis was too soon wearing thin.

I must have dozed, for the next thing I remember was the hostess gently touching my shoulder and saying, "San Fernando de Apure—*cinco minutos.*" Here was some Spanish I could understand, and I bolted up. We were flying now at about five hundred feet. There was water everywhere beneath, yet this wasn't a sea. I was looking down on a curious mixture of grass and flood—high green grass extending up over quiet water. Here and there lagoons, scummed around the edges with floating swamp vegetation, had the appearance of haphazardly thrown jigsaw pieces; some were connected with squeezing and contort-

The State of Apure lies at the heart of Venezuela's great inland plains or llanos. Here, a mere 7° above the Equator, the year has only two seasons: six hot months of dryness, six hot months of rain and flood.

ing channels; each was a mirror reflecting the dark, ugly rain clouds under which we were flying. We were approximately two hundred miles inland from the north coast of South America.

The plane began banking and I caught a glimpse close below of a broad ribbon of water, then low rooftops, as we straightened out and began rapidly to descend. The wheels thumped, and in a few seconds we were taxiing as though over a bumpy country road. Spray streamed past my window, and when the motors finally stopped I saw that the plastic glass was diagramed with rivulets of mud. "San Fernando de Apure," the hostess called out again. As I made my way to the now open door I felt a draft of damp, tepid air. Outside the door hung a curtain of straight pelting rain. Two passengers were behind me in the aisle; the rest, apparently, were continuing equatorward. The plane was to stop here for only a few minutes.

Someone out on the muddy ground was carrying on a conversation in shouts with the pilot who had opened his cockpit window. Another man materialized through the downpour, shoving a small disembarking platform to the doorframe where I stood. I hesitated, then dashed down the steps and started running, as most people do when caught in a shower. Already half soaked, I checked myself. Where was I running? My glasses needed wiping, but I made out a cluster of open-sided field sheds some distance off and bent for them, splashing and skidding through warm mud puddles.

I ducked in under the nearest of the sheds, and straightened up to find myself confronted with a living armamentarium. The man, a good head shorter than I, had on an enormous upsweeping officer's cap that seemed to equalize our heights. A revolver showed in the holster on his hip, and his belt was bristling with cartridges. He fired some Spanish at me and waited. *"No hablo Español,"* I said, much at a loss, and started to wipe my glasses. There was more Spanish from him, rapid and insistent, so I pulled my passport and assorted papers from my briefcase. He took them, turned and marched over to a rustic counter near by. One sheet after another he paged, one envelope after another he opened, the frown on his face seeming to grow sterner, for these papers were mostly in English. Two rifle-carrying soldiers had meanwhile appeared.

Suddenly the papers stopped rattling. The man with the *Wehrmacht* hat had come to a letter written in Spanish by the Venezuelan Ambassador in Washington requesting that the bearer, I, be treated with respect and courtesy while searching for the scarlet ibis in Venezuela. The nail of the man's forefinger reverently scratched across the great seal of Venezuela, and a change came over his face. He barked something at his subordinates that worked further facial miracles. They smiled, I smiled; the papers were handed back to me, and in a speech containing a goodly sprinkling of *buenos,* I received what I think was a cordial welcome to San Fernando, capital of the llanos state of Apure.

I learned subsequently that a strong detail of *Guardia Nacional,* or internal security police, was stationed at San Fernando, for there was current talk of revolution in the llanos. Every traveler entering or leaving the area was subject to the closest sort of police scrutiny for hidden arms, papers of defection, etc. It later came to my ears that the inspector, upon reading the ambassadorial letter, had surmised that I was on international political business and that Scarlet Ibis was code for something secret and very important.

Scarlet Ibis did stand for something very important—if only to me. It had been a full year earlier, when on a casual visit to the Bronx Park Zoo in New York City, that I had come upon a placard attached to the wire screening of the zoo's great outdoor aviary. On the placard were small sketches to aid the zoo visitor in the quick identification of the various bird species free to wander about the enclosure or to sit on the branches there. Each sketch was accompanied by the bird's common and technical names, as well as a statement of its geographical range.

One of the listings, "Scarlet Ibis, *Guara rubra*," and the adjacent sketch depicting a solid-red bird caught my interest. I scanned the aviary's population, but could find no bird having plumage anywhere near that color. It was not color but rather profile that finally attracted me to a certain shin-high creature poking away at something or other on the ground. It was a sad-looking bird, with thin, stilted legs, feathers of palest pink and a long arced-down beak that looked comically out of proportion to the rest of the body. The profile and general form of this forsaken one corresponded to the sketch—but where was the scarlet?

How a passing incident or a chance observation may initiate a complex course of human action is a subject relished by those inclined toward a fatalistic view. Or, as in this instance, how a discrepancy between the color of a living bird and that of its picture was eventually to lead me from the ordered life of a research scientist in New York onto the flooded plains of central Venezuela in the role of a Jason could be a case in point. My eyes turned back to the placard and I read in an explanatory note there that, although the scarlet ibis in its natural habitat is bright red, its molt replacements in captivity are invariably pallid. The explanation in itself was satisfactory, but next day, seeking a fuller acquaintance with this creature whose color idiosyncrasy had diverted me, I found myself in the Public Library at Fifth Avenue and 42nd Street, where the second link of a curious reaction chain was to be forged.

The literature I uncovered painted the scarlet ibis in the wild as among the most elegantly hued of birds. These descriptions were aged, recorded by single travelers, missionaries, early naturalists. So extravagant a word picture I had rarely come across. One observer adjectivally exceeded the next:

Edwards, 1847: ". . . scarlet livery of dazzling beauty . . ."

Leotaud, 1866: ". . . beautiful red stains on a green background . . ."

Penard, 1908: ". . . mangroves as if spattered with blood . . ."

Beebe, 1910: ". . . flaming with a brilliance which shamed any pigment of human art . . ."

Dawson, 1917: ". . . once seen, never forgotten . . ."

I had occasion, some time after this session of provocative reading, to visit with officials of the National Geographic Society in Washington, D. C. During the course of our discussion of other matters I happened to mention the pale-pink bird I had seen in the Bronx Park Zoo and those rhapsodic descriptions of the species in the wild. Dr. John Oliver La Gorce, at that time vice-president, now president, of the Society, seemed interested, so later I compiled all my library findings in the form of a brief report, which I submitted to the society's Research Committee. In my covering letter I pointed out how about thirty years ago the scarlet ibis had rather mysteriously vanished from the printed record; I suggested that perhaps this would be something worth investigating. I had previously published a minor natural-history article in the *Geographic,* and Dr. La Gorce was acquainted with my avocational interest in photography.

Not long afterward I received in the mails a formal invitation from the National Geographic Society to organize, under its sponsorship, an expedition to South America for the purpose of seeking out the scarlet ibis in its native breeding haunts and there on the spot of recording its hues on modern color film. Without hesitation I accepted, arranging for a leave of absence from my laboratory. And with that, the chain's third link was added.

My reading had defined the bird's range as extending along a 2,000-mile arc from Brazil, through the Guianas and Venezuela, to Colombia (with occasional storm-blown stragglers reported as far north as the Gulf coast of Mexico); its habitat—river estuaries, coastal mud flats, inland swamps. But the giant northeast shoulder of South America is an imposing area in which to locate a forgotten bird not much larger than a pigeon. Had I known that the species was still abundant there I might simply have flown to, say, Georgetown, British Guiana, or to Para, Brazil, or to Maracaibo, Venezuela, and asked the first person I met where the scarlet birds were to be found. But there was something about the way the scarlet ibis had dropped sheer out of the bird literature that put me on guard against any so precipitate a move. Could the absence of a modern ornithological study imply that the species was no longer abundant, perhaps that it was facing the same man-versus-nature threat that had decimated so many another conspicuously colored bird?

My inquiries at length brought me in touch with William H. Phelps of Caracas, Venezuela, a specialist on the birds of northern South America. Born in New York and graduated from Harvard, Phelps as a young man had gone to Venezuela, the then land of opportunity. He had become a naturalized Venezuelan, as well as very rich. Since boyhood, birds—collecting, studying and classifying them— had been his hobby; of late years (he was approaching seventy-two) birds were virtually his profession. The *Coleccion Ornitologica Phelps,* a study collection of bird skins maintained in Caracas, is perhaps the best of its kind in South America.

I recall the day Phelps and I first talked Scarlet Ibis. We stood at the drawing-room windows of his hotel quarters high above Central Park South in New York City. Below us the park's pathways were dotted with late-afternoon strollers. The sight was spectacular, and one that has caused many a visitor to New York to gasp, but our concern was with the swamps and jungles of tropical South America. As we talked, my fancy led me across hot rain-pelted mud flats along the coast where the Orinoco's mouth yawns; through mangrove snarls on the island of Marajó where the Amazon flows into the Atlantic; into the mosquito-clouded mouth of the Pomeroon River in British Guiana. Since the zoo encounter, I had allowed the scarlet ibis to pass from the narrow realm of colored birds; gradually it had become the symbol of hidden places and the heavy beauty of the tropics.

Phelps affirmed that along the Venezuelan coast scarlet ibises had once been as plentiful as sea gulls, but that Venezuela is no longer the wilderness of thirty years ago. Now oil is king, cities have mushroomed, commerce and industry flourish, progress is the keynote. So of course, Phelps commented dryly, as though one phenomenon were the unquestioned corollary of the other, the scarlet ibis is not so abundant as it once was. On the other hand, he said in the next breath, Venezuelan urbanity and industrialism are limited to a relatively small portion of the country. There are still enormous reaches of unexplored primeval wilderness extending southward from the coast into the great basin of the Orinoco. He believed that Venezuela still harbored concentrations of breeding scarlet ibises; but exactly where—that was the question.

Phelps and I had been corresponding for months previous to this meeting. He had already sent letters of inquiry to people he knew who lived in various far-flung outposts—in the Orinoco jungles, near coastal swamps and river deltas, in the highlands. And to San Fernando de Apure, in the middle of the immense llanos plains, he had dispatched his most experienced field collector to make an on-the-spot reconnaissance. Phelps assured me that within a month he would have concrete information about the scarlet ibis.

Not long after his return to Caracas I received an air-mail letter bearing the glad news that his collector, a Señor Urbano, had located a *garcero,* or breeding colony, of about 100 scarlet ibises on a tributary of the Apure River about 200 miles south of Caracas. The Phelps collector had learned further that such llanos water birds nest only during the wet season when rivers swell and overflow the land. However, this particular garcero was only five hours upstream from the city of San Fernando and hence could easily be reached. If I would plan my expedition for the coming September or October, I would in all probability meet with success.

This letter dissolved any fears that the species had become a rarity. I would merely fly to a little town in central Venezuela called San Fernando de Apure, proceed upriver a few hours by dugout, and there come upon the fabulously hued scarlet ibis. The expedition would start out with a personnel of one—myself. Along the way I would pick up native helpers, guides, boatmen, as needed. The logistic problem here in New York was relatively simple: a few such obvious prerequisites as a tarpaulin, a photographic blind, an outboard motor, all of which would be sent ahead by air freight, and a stock of clothes and personal effects. In view of the proximity of the birds to my probable hotel base in San Fernando, there would be no food or camp problems. Nevertheless, I visited an army-surplus store in New York and bought one of those hammocks advertised as used during the jungle warfare in the South Pacific. All purpose and all weather, the ad said, hang it anywhere in the bush and forget about rain, mosquitoes and vermin.

One evening early that following September I quietly took a bus to La Guardia Field and was off on the regular overnight plane to Venezuela. I stayed awake most of the night studying a Spanish grammar.

Each step toward my goal seemed more comfortable than the last. Within twelve smooth flying hours I disembarked at the Maiquetía Airfield near La Guaira on the north coast of Venezuela, where Mr. Phelps met and saw me through customs, then into his limousine and off.

Caracas, Venezuela's urbane capital, southward into the mountains, must wait. We would spend the week end in coastal Macuto, where Phelps's son Billy—a follower in his father's ornithological footsteps, and himself an authority on Venezuelan birds—had a seaside villa.

Billy, who has the look of a Wall Street executive but the animated mannerisms of an indigenous Latin, took my scarlet-ibis quest quite as seriously as did his father. But if my project had not rested solidly on the Urbano report, I should have been a little disquieted, for neither Billy nor his father, they re-emphasized, had actually ever seen nesting scarlet ibises in Venezuela. Most of their ornithological field work had been done during the dry summer months when roads and trails are open—a logical time for studying many tropical species, but not water birds of the ibis, heron and egret class. These nest only during the Venezuelan winter when the rains come and the coastal marshes and inland plains are deeply flooded. I know Billy did not mean to be discouraging when he added that, of course, no one goes to the llanos in the hot and fluvial winter. Human life there slows then to a near standstill or takes sleepily to the hammock, mosquitoes swarm, visitors stay away. Furthermore, the garceros are located only in the most inaccessible spots. Good luck Urbano had found one so close to San Fernando, Billy added, probably noting the slight drop of my jaw.

"I've arranged a little dinner party in Caracas for tomorrow night," Billy told me. "Gustavo Ramella Vegas will be there. He knows the llanos better than I, and he has been there in winter."

Tomorrow night came. Dinner was over, liqueurs set aside, and the guests made their way across the indoor patio garden to the library. Mainly for my benefit Señor Ramella had brought along a color reel of his various tiger-hunting trips to the llanos. Ramella, a Caracas business-man, frequently flies his plane to whatever place in the llanos he and his friends think the shooting is best. They rarely return without several handsome pelts of *el tigre*. The llanos big cats are actually jaguars, but considered to be as fierce and unrelenting as true Asiatic tigers. When-ever Billy Phelps hears that Ramella has bagged another half-dozen tigers, he good-humoredly throws up his hands and argues conservation. Ramella replies that llanos cattle-men are grateful for his hunting. For every pound of tiger killed, Ramella insists, Venezuela has a hundred extra pounds of beef for its tables or markets.

"In the film," Ramella had told me at dinner, "you will see a scarlet ibis—but only from afar, for they are shy and only a few times have they come within my camera range. They make their nests in the middle of swamps with water all around. You will not find it easy to locate them without an airplane." His remarks did not bother me, in view of the Urbano information.

The movie was shown. I caught a glimpse of red in some marsh vegetation. It was on the screen for only a second or two, and I could not tell whether it was bird, flower or Kodachrome artifact. But there was one episode in the movie that was conclusive. The scene was a llanos river-bank. An eel, five or six feet long and caught by someone with a baited line, had surfaced and was being pulled in toward shore. Suddenly the water around the eel splashed in a dozen places, and almost immediately red blood could be seen pouring from as many places in the eel's skin. "Caribes," confirmed Señor Ramella above the sound of the projector. Synchronously with the appearance of blood in the water, the attack reached a frenzied pitch. In hundreds now, it seemed, these hand-sized razor-toothed fish hurled themselves at the helpless eel body, each accomplishing a series of deep, clean, flesh removals. Quickly, before our eyes, the eel was consumed; then the water was still.

I had read stories, all hair-raising, about these so-called flesh eaters of the South American tropics: a canoeist, trailing his hand in the water, feels a sting, then finds the stump of a finger spouting blood; a man falls into a river and is converted within a short time into a skeleton; one of Bolívar's armies wading across a llanos stream is demoralized by caribes; a careless river bather emerges from the water screaming and toeless. The caribe of Venezuela, the piranha of Brazil, the perai of British Guiana—all belong to a genus of small fresh-water fish reputed to be the most ferocious of its size in the world. When the naturalist Humboldt described the caribe as "one of the greatest scourges of these climes," he was specifically referring to the Apure River Basin where my scarlet ibises were awaiting me.

Within an hour after my welcome to Apure by the airfield constabulary I had checked in at my hotel and was abroad in the quaint inland town of San Fernando—muddy in winter, dusty in summer. As black is to white was this new world to the one I had just left. Gone were the elegance of Macuto, the modernity of Caracas. Gone were the desert dryness of the coast, the freshness of the mountains. Here in September in the middle of the llanos the atmosphere was heavy and dank, the sky low-hanging and sullen and ever on the verge of tears.

This character of air and sky reflected moodily from the

faces I saw—somber faces, even the children's. Iberia was
in them, also Africa and aboriginal America. Sharp black
eyes, skins varying from light to dark brown, high cheek-
bones, bent noses—these were features I saw, pulled from
three great races. Here in the llanos, where a century
earlier Bolívar's armies had campaigned in the War for
Independence, "race purity" had long since gone by the
board. Shaken together and well mixed were the genes of
those with whom I rubbed shoulders as I passed down
those narrow streets lined with low whitewashed walls.

My first objective in this town of 12,000 was to locate
a man whose name was Marcos Delgado, the river guide
who had taken Urbano up the Río Apure and into the
tributary Portuguesa to the garcero of red birds. Directions
supplied by Urbano through Phelps indicated that Delgado
lived near the Kiosko Regional, a store by the town's municipal river wharf. There, as Urbano had done a year
earlier, my plan was to arrange with Delgado for guidance
and transportation upriver so that a preliminary examination of the bird site could be made. Later I would rent my
own boat and hire my own field assistants.

The municipal wharf was not difficult to find, for, as
in most tropical river towns, it was at the center of things.
The markets, the public square, the saddle shops, the
loafers, the open-air eating and drinking places lay close
around, no more than a few feet above the level of the
river.

At my first unobstructed view of the river, thoughts of
Marcos Delgado were momentarily forgotten. This river,
this Río Apure, was no river; it was a monster. Pictures of
it I had seen in the States had shown a modest stream
quietly meandering through a sand gully. But I had seen

no pictures of the Apure during the wet season. This was the height of the floods—September—and here swirling, simmering, pushing, bulging, a good quarter-mile across from threatened bank to threatened bank, was the Apure at crest. I stood there fascinated as by a serpent.

The river was the color of the gloomy overcast. But out in the main channel, sweeping downstream, were patches of bright-green vegetation—floating gardens of bluish blooming hyacinths—torn from grassy marshes and swamps through which the waters had passed on their way to San Fernando and bound now for the Orinoco a hundred miles to the east. The Apure is to the llanos of central Venezuela what the Missouri is to our prairie states. Its hundreds of swollen veins with their thousands of full capillaries drain the torrential winter rainfall that would otherwise create a permanent inland sea of the llanos. Only a foot or so higher than the present level, and there would be trouble for cattle already sequestered on the little remaining un-flooded land; and for riverbank peons it would be a time for prayers.

It occurred to me with suddenness that only by braving these sweeping waters would I be able to attain my goal. The Apure current was an obstacle on which I had not altogether figured, and feebly I began to wonder whether I should not wait until December when the river would recede before setting out for the garcero. But the scarlet ibis, a water bird, is patterned to breed and nest only during the wet season. If I postponed my work until the rains stopped and the floods abated, I would find only empty and deserted nests.

It is a familiar experience in life to be acquainted with the facts of a situation without truly comprehending them.

In Caracas, Billy Phelps had made a point of the size and force of the Apure and the Orinoco during the height of the flood season; and I had read statistics on the rise, fall, maximum width, depth and volume of these rivers. But it took a sentient dimension to convert those facts into reality.

This wharf on which I stood, half mesmerized, was designed in such a way as to accommodate the seasonal risings and fallings of the river. It was a series of solid concrete step-downs, like the side of an Aztec temple, so that canoes could discharge passengers or cargo, irrespective of the water level. Many canoes were there now, unloading bananas, yams, cheese. They were floating not far below the top step.

These wooden dugouts, the chief means of winter transportation in the llanos, were long and slim, like pencils. I watched the apparent ease with which they were maneuvered in and out of the swift Apure channel, slicing through the water under power of droning outboards, some not long off American assembly lines. I recalled my assumption in New York that mine would be the only up-to-date motor in the llanos. New to these sights, I half expected any moment to see one or all of the speeding dugouts roll over and disappear into the ugly water. But there were no capsizings, no screams of drowning men. Nevertheless, I did not care to think that onto such a craft I must affix my little 10-hp Sea-Horse for the five-hour trip upstream to the birds. Upstream, against that current. I turned away; the need for Delgado never had seemed more urgent.

The proprietor of the Kiosko Regional pointed to a row of hovels not far removed from the wharf, smelly little dirt-floored places where rivermen hang their hammocks when in port. I canvassed them all, and it was neither a pleasant

nor successful undertaking. My Spanish was rarely understood. At best the name Delgado would get some reaction
to the effect that he had not been seen for weeks, and no
one seemed able to provide information as to where he
might be reached. To idlers along the wharf and to men
unloading dugouts, I tried mentioning *coro-coro* (the llanos
name for scarlet ibis), pointing inquiringly up the river.
The answer I got was either a look of silent distrust or a
flat *"Yo no sé."*

I sought no food that evening. Instead I went directly to
my hotel and inside to its *sala*, or common sleeping room.
I was withered by the day's events and, following a well-
known escapist pattern, hoped to sleep deeply and leave
my troubles behind.

This cattle-town hotel, which I shall call the Grande,
was different in several major respects from hotels of northern convention: first, there were no beds. As a remarkable
vindication of an earlier hunch, sleep was to be achieved in
my own hammock, which during the afternoon someone
had obligingly removed from its case and hung from two
opposing wall hooks. Other hammocks were strung in the
same room. These were of light white cotton or palm fiber
and draped with mosquito netting. One was already occupied—an early sleeper, perhaps an escapist like myself.
Another was just being entered by a short, stout man who
glanced quickly at me, then at my hammock, then politely
away again. Politely, for this hammock—the same that I
had bought at the army-surplus store and had never seen
rigged—was, in the sala of this provincial hotel, a thing to
behold.

Designed to be rainproof, sunproof, windproof, mosquitoproof and snakeproof, this creation was of processed green nylon, with a full-fledged roof. You crawled in through a slit in the side netting, then closed the slit by means of a long rustproof zipper. Once there, you were proofed against everything but discomfort. For centuries people of the South American llanos and bush country have slept, siestaed, procreated and died in their simple woven hammocks. This contraption of mine could have adequately subserved only the latter function.

For hours I lay there tossing to find a comfortable position, the subject of Delgado meanwhile taking on typical nighttime distortion. In reality I had yet little cause for despair. The garcero existed, of that there could be no question. I could draw a map showing its position; it even had a name, *Carral,* and it lay conspicuously off the Caño Ruende, which is a small tributary of the Río Portuguesa, which is a large tributary of the Río Apure, which is an even larger tributary of the Río Orinoco. If Delgado had died, left town or was off on a protracted spree, I could certainly find some other riverman and charter some other dugout. But initial disappointment, fatigue and the gloom of night, not to mention the effect of being in a strange land amid people of a strange tongue—all these tended in my imagination to turn a momentary impasse into a threatening situation.

Also abetting my wakefulness were the night sounds of the sala. Four men were sharing this room with me. One, sleepless like myself, lighted a cigarette; by the brief eerie glow of the match through the netting I could see the other three hammocks now hanging low and heavy, their occupants breathing audibly and making frequent unpleasant sleep noises. Finally the smoker got up and made a trip to the adjoining yard where there was a privy. He stumbled over a sleeping pig whose grunts fused with human snores and rumblings. Mosquitoes, allegedly malarial, droned as they foolishly sought to penetrate my GI bower.

My mood became conceivably that of a man who, having leaped from a high window, wonders whether he should have done so. I did not have to be here: my laboratory in New York was a well-ordered place where cells under the microscope were silent, where test tubes and reagent bottles were decorous; my bed at home had foam rubber laid on a box spring; my living room overlooked the East River, which never flooded. There was no economic motive. I would not have had to accept the National Geographic Society's invitation to go into the bush of South America in quest of an obscure bird.

Well, then, why was I here? Patently, to seek the scarlet ibis; but there was more.

The question of what, at core, motivates men to do what they do is as complex as life itself. Most often the springs that actuate human conduct are hidden in depths far below the limit of self-examination to reveal, but at times some are sufficiently close to the surface to be at least partially recognized and identified. In my own case, as a scientist involved primarily in laboratory aspects of research biology, I have periodically felt the urge (not an uncommon one these days) to throw off the astringent cloak of specialization. I have wished to approach biological processes as they occur in open nature; I have wished to see, watch, sense anew, reflect.

This may imply a factor of escape—not necessarily the desire to run away from any specific odium but away from the lull of the familiar, from the routine and humdrum.

Much human activity has this component, often intermingled with a vague longing, sometimes a pressing need, for that which will stir the resting senses. The scarlet ibis, as the material object of my quest, was as much a means as an end.

Too, when a year earlier at the Bronx Park Zoo my eyes had contrasted that caged bird with the sketch of a wild one, an implication there, involving confinement versus freedom, may have appealed to subconscious susceptibilities, bringing influence to bear on an already existing interest in nature lore and a liking for tropical climes derived from earlier travels. Finally, one of the elements leading to my present difficulties may have been simply the promise of beauty. There was a creation somewhere in the tropical fastnesses of South America that I wanted to see.

It was abundantly evident now that, for the fulfillment of these aspirations, I would have to pay a price.

Only when rain began to thunder down on the corrugated tin roof and spatter on the mud of the courtyard were the day's inauspicious events forgotten, the ruminations shelved, the motivations accepted, the unsoothing sounds masked—and, hammock be damned, I was able to sleep.

Morning was announced violently by a cock just outside the always open doorway to the sala. Three weeks later, after I had become inured somewhat to llanos ways and facilities, I returned to this same hotel and found it a colorful place to live. But that first morning I was a bit startled by some of life's naked realisms. At this point I had no idea of personal procedures in a hotel whose sole water source was an iron faucet at one side of the yard and whose latrine was equipped with only a seatless, flushless cement hole over which to squat. I decided to lie low in my jungle nest and learn from my confreres.

One by one the sleepers tumbled out of their hammocks. The first put on his pants and sandals, slopped across the mud patio to the privy; on the way back he picked up a well-chipped washbasin, drew a little water from the faucet and placed the basin on a stand near the single dining table just outside the sala door. A few splashes, a face-wiping on a used towel that hung from a nail on one of the uprights supporting the low tin roof, then the wash water was flung out into the yard, aimed at a hen who squawked away noisily. Next, the man sat down at the table, where a minute or two later a buxom, barefooted servant girl served what I assumed was coffee. Two pigs grunted in the mud only a few feet away and chickens strolled boldly under the table, occasionally depositing droppings. Then the other guests followed much the same routine; one shaved in a small rectangular mirror that hung on the stud next to the towel. There was little talk.

The day starts early in the llanos, for by midafternoon all work must be out of the way so that serious eating, drinking and siestaing may begin. Accordingly, these men (llanos drummers and traveling salesmen, I learned) had soon left the hotel. Remaining in my hammock, I watched the enormously corpulent manageress waddling barefoot about the veranda and gabbing with the maid. The two looked in and, seeing my hammock still occupied, carried on a long conversation in which the word *norteamericano* was repeated several times. Then they went on to other things, and I got up.

The latrine hole was no source of assurance to me. Seepage from it to the yard's mud where the pigs wallowed was inevitable; and the damp cement floor of both sala and dining veranda, on which men, women, pigs and chickens tracked latrine-soaked ooze, would have been a delight to any parasitologist. Likewise, the common basin and towel struck me as an extraordinarily efficient spreader of micro-fauna and -flora. There was a small porcelain filter mechanism attached to a second faucet in the yard from which *aqua pura* for drinking dripped into a pail; the "filtered" water was coming through a crack rather than through the pores of the porcelain. But at least momentarily there were no mosquitoes or rain, and I had been well immunized against typhoid in the States. Furthermore, I was not here in the llanos on a public-health mission or on a study of provincial customs. If this was winter life in the llanos, I was determined to see its charms. So resolved, I stepped out of the hotel a half hour later and into the street for a second try at San Fernando. I had not bothered to shave.

San Fernando is laid out in checkerboard design. A few of its streets are paved curb to curb, but most of them have only two ribbons of cement wide enough and spaced to accommodate the wheels of an oxcart or automobile—and woe to any vehicle that slips off into the mud in the middle or on either side. Closing in hard from both sides of each street, and margined by a high narrow walkway, are the conjoining white walls of residences and small shops. Eaves of corrugated tin or heavy tiling extend out over the walk and are so low that anyone of average height must often stoop. Windows and doors of residences are usually closed; on the inside, unseen from the street, each house has a quadrangular veranda surrounding a little courtyard.

Within these porchless blank-front walls lives San Fernando's middle class. The poor, I observed later, live in hovels on the town's outskirts; the rich prefer Caracas.

My course led eventually across the central plaza, then into a side street where I found the general store of Señor M. A. Mazerhane, Billy Phelps's commercial representative in San Fernando, to whom I carried a letter of introduction. This I had not expected to use, but now, in view of the Delgado situation, there was no choice. Mazerhane was in Caracas at the time, but his partner, Señor Toufic, a Venezuelan of Turkish extraction, received me.

"Coro-coros?" he puzzled. He read the letter carefully, and then rattled a rather long paragraph in my direction. I could not understand what he was saying, but I sensed that it added up to: sorry, sir, I know nothing about birds. He summoned one of his clerks, gave some instructions, then turned back to his account books. The clerk, a young man in a white-duck jacket buttoned up to the chin, beckoned me to follow as he stepped out of the store. Back again across the plaza he led me, and into one narrow street after another. Several shops we passed looked like miniature garages; instead of cars inside, there were outboards, dozens of them, neatly racked along the back walls. Some were disassembled, with mechanics at work on them.

Eventually, in the outskirts of town, we came to a small house at whose door the clerk from Mazerhane's pounded vigorously. A crack appeared; someone within listened to the extensive and rather formal speech being delivered. Then the door opened full and the merry-eyed man there spoke to me: "My speak English wery well. You require a translator? At your service."

A few words of English—the first since Caracas—came

like a sunrise. Seeing my pleasure, the clerk excused himself and left me with my new acquaintance.

"I am seeking a man by the name of Marcos Delgado, who lives near the Kiosko Regional," I said. "I wish to employ him as a guide to take me to the garcero called Carral, off the Río Portuguesa."

"Ah. You wish to collect egret plumes."

"No. I seek a red bird known as the coro-coro."

"Ah." There was a long interval of thought, then: "But you are come at the wrong time. The coro-coro comes in the *verano*—how you say, summer?—when the water goes and there is no rain. Wherever remains a small pond, come all the birds of the llanos—white, red and blue. But now is *invierno,* winter, and there is no coro-coro—only herons and egrets nesting in the garceros." This was a new variant on scarlet-ibis natural history.

I explained the basis for my belief that coro-coros also nest in garceros, at least in the one off the Portuguesa. My Urbano-Delgado story drew only a shrug of the shoulders. I told who I was and where from. Delighted to meet a *norteamericano;* fine little country you have up there, the man said with no humor intended. He himself had learned the beautiful English language while working in Trinidad as a youth. Now, permanently a resident of San Fernando, he followed the profession of musician. He often took his little band of five to villages up and down the river to play at fiestas; of course, not now when the water was high— only in summertime. He would be glad to help me in any way he could. First, let us go and make more inquiries about Delgado; there were others, too, that might shed some light.

The man's views on the breeding habits of birds I was

willing to disregard, but his ability to speak at least rudimentary English filled my heart with joy. For the moment there in San Fernando the language frustration was dissolved, and with my new friend, Miguel Siso, I headed toward the center of town, back to the wharf and the Kiosko Regional, the site of my previous day's wanderings and difficulties.

A bubbling, effusive chap, Señor Siso directed me to sit at an outdoor table not far from where the Apure wetted its temple steps, then clapped his hands for service from the concession near by. *"Dos cervezas,"* he ordered of a barefoot gamin who came running up.

The beers were brought. My friend polished his off quickly and ordered two more. We chatted about everything but coro-coros. Siso was well known apparently, for almost every passer-by greeted him. Finally with his thirst quenched and manner relaxed, my friend said, "Now I will ask these *baquianos*—how you say, rivermen?—about Delgado."

Grateful to get down to business, I followed Siso as he made his way among the shirtless sweating men lounging there along the river front. With about every third man he went into a huddle during which a torrential exchange in Spanish took place. Then to the little shop called the Kiosko Regional for another series of interviews. Then more walkings up and down the wharfside, more talk, more shouting down to men at work loading or unloading canoes. Sometimes there was laughter and much amusement, and sharp eyes would be upon me.

Finally Siso turned. "With Delgado you will have no luck. We must search elsewhere for learn about the coro-coros. Come, let us have another cerveza, then I take you to a friend who knows much about animals. He has a pet babo."

Perhaps it was the beer, perhaps it was because the sidewalks were narrow; in any case, we two proceeded down the street's cement ribbons, a man on each. The important Delgado link was manifestly lost from my chain of plans, but to have found someone willing conceivably to map a new way for me I accepted as a bit of good fortune, and hopefully I followed him.

My first reward for thus bestowing faith lay in learning how to execute the provincial Venezuelan equivalent of a handshake. When two friends meet or when two people are introduced, one places his right hand on the other's left shoulder, and vice versa. The amount of patting and the degree of lingering reflect the warmth of the greeting. It is actually a very pleasant custom, and carries a greater potential for expressing shades of feeling than does our Anglo-Saxon shaking of hands. Previously, while we were sitting at the riverside *cervecería* or ranging the wharf, there had been no introductions. But friendship had ripened, and now whenever Siso met an acquaintance I would immediately be introduced as *"Un científico muy distinguido de norteamerica."* Remembering the beer, I forgave the exaggeration and enthusiastically exchanged shoulder pats with the man to whom I was being presented.

This ceremony must have been repeated at least a half-dozen times before we arrived at an open doorway leading into someone's living room. In we went, without knock or announcement, and passed through to an inside courtyard with a perimeter of sky-lighted ground-level verandas. An elderly man appeared who greeted my friend as though he were a long-lost brother. I was presented, and there was again more patting of shoulders.

The courtyard—muddy like everything else in these parts not covered by cement—was graced by a number of small trees and bushes. Perched there on the branches were a dozen or so parrots and parakeets and a pair of rainbowed macaws—also several small monkeys watching us intently. In the middle of the yard lay what I thought was a sarcophagus. Noting my stare, our host took my arm and urged me over to see what was, in fact, a concrete tank about ten feet long, two feet wide and with walls a good eight inches thick. It was half full of soupy green water from whose surface bulged a length of scaly hide. In a second I saw the hide was that of an all but submerged member of the crocodile family (the babo!), whose body seemed to fill the inner length and width of the tank. A nostriled snout protruded from the green slime; eyes farther back had an unfathomable expression.

While I gaped, Señor Siso supplied the explanation. Years ago our nature-loving host had caught the animal while it was quite small, depositing it, for reasons not stated, in this aqua-mausoleum. At first a cover had been used to prevent the captive's escape. But of late years the babo, well fed by its master, had become so nicely domesticated that the cover was no longer necessary. The man demonstrated his pet's fine appetite by holding a hunk of meat close to its nostrils. There was a single brief, sickening thud, a splash, and the meat was gone.

"There are many crocodiles here in the llanos," Siso commented, "many of size larger than this one. When you go close to riverbanks you must take care. They will upset your canoe and eat you." He wasn't joking. He went on to explain that in the past, before commercial hide interests moved in, crocodiles, alligators, caimans had been as plentiful as herons along the Apure. The methods of organized skinning crews had involved herding hundreds, thousands, of these reptiles into a river cul-de-sac and there slaughtering them. Today the crocodile family is not nearly so teeming here, but one must still keep his eyes open when near tall grass close to the river. My feelings toward the Río Apure were not warmed by this information.

Following a well-established Latin amenity, we made no mention of the purpose of our visit until we were comfortably seated on veranda hammocks and a servant had brought coffee. I knew finally that the subject close to my heart had come up when the word *coro-coro* appeared for the first time in the jumble of fast Spanish talk.

Suddenly Siso leaped up out of his hammock and patted our host fervently with both hands on both shoulders. Then he turned to me, beaming. "You need not Delgado. You need not the garcero. Here! *Sí!* Here in San Fernando is the coro-coro! This man he tell this. Come, we go. Ah!" He seized me by the arm and hurried me away.

A shower caught us halfway down the block and we ducked under the tin awning of a little saddle shop. While we waited, Siso beamed in cryptic silence. "You will see, señor, you will see" was all he would say. I turned and examined the holstered knives, the saddles, the lariats and horse blankets.

The splattering outside stopped and we were off again, past the barracks of the *Guardia Nacional,* past a school with a lettered quotation from Bolívar above its door, then into a low section of town partly inundated by river spill-

age, where several houses had canoes tied to their door-
steps. Finally in a drier section, we entered a house with a
courtyard somewhat like the one we had just left. No sarcophagus here, but a large wire coop of the sort suitable
for chickens. As a matter of fact, there *were* chickens
scratching there in the mud, along with several sad-looking
shin-high birds with long curved-down beaks and pale-pink
feathers.

"There you have coro-coros!" announced my friend,
pointing to the birds, and pleased as punch to have helped
el norteamericano achieve the object of his quest so easily.

Chapter 2

WHOEVER SAID that the fun of life is reaching for a goal, not the actual attainment, had never done much reaching over the flooded llanos of central Venezuela.

Some such cynicism may have been passing through my mind as, two weeks after my momentous discovery of those domesticated scarlet ibises in the San Fernando hen coop, I stepped out of a dirty dugout and onto a slippery mudbank at Arichuna, a village on the Apure River about thirty miles east of San Fernando. I needed no mirror to tell me that the eager, clean-shaven look which I had brought to the llanos a seeming century before had suffered some deterioration. The store look had long since departed from my khaki trousers, and an indifference toward mosquitoes, flies and mud had grown to be part of my manner. The naked urchins, the yapping, bony dogs and the sprinkling of adult idlers watching on the riverbank that darkening evening at Arichuna seemed unaware that one of the people hopping out of the dugout was no true llanero, although a perceiving eye might have deduced it from the somewhat deferential treatment I seemed to be getting from my companions.

We had left the capital city around noon on what, according to my llanos notes, constituted the tenth distinct field sortie I had made thus far in my search for native scarlet ibises and their breeding haunts. For some inscruta-

46

ble reason the *rara avis* has a habit of being even rarer when it is specifically sought. Those scarlet ibises found the year before on the Caño Ruende upstream five hours from San Fernando, and upon whose presence there my entire expedition had hinged, were missing when within three days after my arrival from Caracas Señor Siso and I, through the services of an alternate guide, had made our way up the Apure and the Portuguesa, into the Caño Ruende and finally to that garcero. The marsh there was alive with snowy white egrets and dusky blue herons, thousands of them, but not one scarlet bird.

The details of that abortive and disappointing trip need not be recorded, nor those of many other sorties in as many other directions. Let it be said only that the Ruende trip relieved me of any notions I may have had regarding the quick and easy availability of nesting scarlet ibises in the Venezuelan llanos. To be sure, the birds had been there a year before; a peon living not far from the garcero told us he had seen them himself and remembered Urbano's visit. But during the current nesting season, the red birds had not returned. As to why, he offered no explanation or theory.

After the Ruende fiasco my business in San Fernando became public knowledge, and an item appeared in the local newspaper telling of my visit, aims and current failure. I became the willing victim of advice givers. Each informant knew exactly where coro-coros were nesting and how to get there. For the most part, their wish to help had no personal-gain motive. So far as I could determine, these good people—peons, rivermen, llaneros—who appeared at my quarters came partly out of curiosity to see what a bird searcher from North America looked like, but mostly to share what each considered to be his exclusive knowledge of Apure bird life. One fellow, the pilot of a dugout that carried cheese from a downriver settlement to San Fernando, said that along his route he passed a certain swamp, and in it, unmistakably, were beautiful nesting scarlet birds. Once a week for the past two months he had come upon them, redder than a steer's blood. I spent two days getting to and from that spot, but the "scarlet" birds turned out to be black-crowned night herons.

Then there were the two peons in a local cervecería who got into an argument and at the pre-blow stage decided to call on me. One said that the red birds nested downriver in a flooded savanna; the other, upriver in a savanna equally flooded. I visited both savannas, but found nothing redder than egrets. There were other volunteer informants, literally dozens of them, all positive they could guide me to the coro-coros. Siso and I sifted such claims, investigated those that seemed anywhere near reasonable, invariably ending up with egrets, herons, anhingas and cormorants, but never with so much as a feather of scarlet.

Then Chico, a llanero, entered the picture. Siso had described him to me as being well known in San Fernando and much respected. His property forty miles to the east on the Río Apure contained one of the largest and most diversely populated garceros in all of Venezuela—certainly a paradise for coro-coros. Chico was in town on a provisioning trip, staying with a city cousin; we would present my calling card and talk with him.

Our talk took place in the usual sort of veranda-lined inside garden. Chico was a younger man than I had expected him to be, small of stature, dark and suspicious of face. He listened intently, looking at me piercingly every now and

Each September and October, at the height of the wet season, the swollen *Río Apure* threatens San Fernando, capital of the llanos State of Apure.

Two cement ribbons pave most streets in San Fernando.

"Coro-coros?" The answer I got was either a look of silent distrust or a flat *"Yo no sé."*

Wooden dugouts are the chief means of winter transportation in the flooded llanos. Their fragility is an illusion.

The wharf at San Fernando is a series of concrete steps, sloped so that canoes and small boats can discharge cargo, irrespective of water level.

The sullen character of rainy season air and sky reflected moodily from the faces I saw.

With the Río Apure at crest, this was a time of waiting; and, should the waters rise a little higher, a time for prayers.

Our woman with the umbrella disembarked in the tall grass, together with the girl and the little child.

*Three of the author's
imperturbable river companions.*

then from under heavy black eyebrows. Siso went on at a great rate for a long while, uninterrupted. When he finished, all was quiet for a moment; then Chico asked in a low tone what Siso translated for me as: "But why does the gentleman wish to find these red birds?"

Siso supplied the answer: how I, *un cientifico*, wanted to study the habits and habitat of the coro-coros and to take pictures of the birds in their natural surroundings. But this did not seem to sit too favorably with Chico, who exhibited no sign whatever of being impressed. An exchange between him and Siso continued, during which the words *las plumas* stood out frequently. Siso told me afterward that Chico at this point had suspected that I was a foreign plume prospector, and he was taking a very dim view of any visit on my part to the garcero.

That he should think of his garcero and its birds largely in terms of the feather trade was not surprising. San Fernando is still full of memories of the halcyon plumage days. In the early 1900s, the era of the plumed hat, feather collecting was big business there—such big business, in fact, that by 1910 snowy and American egrets had been all but cleaned out of the llanos. The record shows that in one year over a million and a half adult birds were butchered in the San Fernando district alone. Collectors got fifteen dollars an ounce and up for prime egret plumes, called "aigrettes" by the trade. In those days a llanos rancher with a garcero on his property either became rich or was exploited by those who did; fortunes with their origins in the grim harvest of egret plumes still exist in Venezuela.

I say grim harvest, for the technique of plume collecting necessitated that the egrets (male or female, since both have identical feathering) be taken only in their full nuptial livery, at a time when the nest-bound young are dependent on parental feeding. The procedure was for armed men to canoe into a flooded garcero and there begin the slaughter. As the gunmen's canoe passed through, the target birds would plummet down off their nests into the water, flapping and foundering there until a second reaper canoe, following closely on the first, would gather them in. The delicate long back plumes would be yanked out and the remains of the bird, often half alive, tossed overboard where the caribes would banquet. For each adult so sacrificed for the adornment of a lady's hat, a full nest of young would starve to death. During this period of their breeding cycle, adult egrets are so obstinately devoted to their young that they can be beaten down off their nests with poles, a practice resorted to when ammunition ran out.

Only when these facts became known to the public in Europe and America did the use of plumes for hat decoration come under censure. The millinery interests insisted to the bitter end that nothing inhuman was involved. They contended that egrets voluntarily shed their plumes during the breeding season and that collectors need but to paddle through a garcero and pick up the floating castoffs—all without harm or disturbance to either adults or young. A bitter natural-history battle, with conservationist and millinery lobbies supplying the ammunition, echoed through the halls of Congress. The issue: does each plumed hat represent several slaughtered birds, or merely the by-product of a natural molting process? Despite furious denials to the contrary, it was finally documented that 90 per cent of all egret plumes collected either in Venezuela or in our own Southern states were taken by the wanton slaughter of nesting birds. The Western Hemisphere egret after only a few years of such organized hunting was approaching the brink of extinction.

Chico knew the facts; he knew also how foreign interests years back had moved in to exploit the local garcero owners. Had the hat with the plumes come back into vogue? Had the statutes been changed? Was I a new variety of the old-time garcero assessor? Again my letters, especially the one from the Venezuelan ambassador which, written in Spanish, Chico could read, had a magical effect. Before the interview ended, Chico was pouring drinks and insisting that I consider his garcero my very own.

But now, what of coro-coros? I pressed. Was Chico acquainted with this bird? Had he ever seen them in his garcero? Were they nesting there this year?

"But of course, señor" was the English equivalent of his reply. "Every year during the floods the coro-coros come. Some years my garcero is so red that it is with difficulty that I keep my bulls from charging it. Never fear, señor. Come with me and you will find what you seek."

Chico was returning to his ranch by boat next morning and, if I would accept his humble hospitality, he would be delighted to have me accompany him. His boat was roomy and I could bring along all my equipment, including my outboard which, incidentally, I had not yet uncrated. In my exploratory river trips so far I had found it expedient to rent dugouts and outboards rather than to activate my own motor.

I know now that there was no connection whatever between my talk with Chico in the afternoon and the arrival at the hotel toward evening of the same day of two men with orders that I report immediately to a certain government office. In a manner that chilled me into believing that a firing squad was ready and waiting, I was told without further explanation that I had failed to register. It is true that all foreigners arriving at an interior town must report to the police, and it is true that I had failed to do so, thinking that my encounter with the constabulary at the airfield had constituted full official compliance and clearance. Hastily I gathered my documents and submitted to being marched down the street to a small building some blocks away where, despite its being late afternoon when no respectable Latin American would be caught at work, two stern-faced men sat behind their small but very bureaucratic desks specifically awaiting my arrival. I did not have Siso there to help me linguistically; but I did have those letters, which, of course, quickly did the trick, and I was released with full apologies.

I relate this incident not as a commentary on any internal political tension that may have existed in Venezuela at that time, but rather because of its possible tie-up with what happened next morning. At eight o'clock I had my things donkey-carted to the wharf where I was to meet Chico. He showed up about ten, wearing an unbelievably big sombrero pulled right down to eye level and held there by a heavy leather chin thong. Two men similarly sombreroed accompanied him. Chico carried a paper bag filled with bottles whose contents at the time I did not guess; one of the men had a shotgun, and the other an armful of ponchos.

They were followed by a noisy crowd of peons driving three donkey carts loaded high with bulging sacks, a standard-size gasoline drum and a miscellaneous assortment of boxes, cans and baskets. I was appalled to realize that all this freight was destined for the dugout tied there to the cement wall. Although considerably larger than the dug-outs in which I had made my earlier river trips, this craft seemed wholly incapable of accepting this amount of cargo, not to mention my own 400-odd pounds of bundles, camera cases, fuel tanks, the crated outboard, etc. Soon the fuel drum was being bounced down the Aztec steps into the dugout, followed by the bags and boxes, and finally my accouterment. A tarp was thrown over the load and the craft now took on the look of a funeral bark. There seemed just enough space left for Chico and me, whom I thought to be the sole passengers. But Chico's two friends also boarded, and then from out of the group of watchers on the bank stepped a young girl together with a woman carrying a closed umbrella and a small child. They squeezed in on one side or the other of the cargo, heaven only knows how; I was to learn shortly that they were not of the expedition but merely friends being given a lift home downriver a few miles. Last, Chico indicated that I board.

I had been studying this jumbo variety of crude hand-hewn dugout, noting, as I had on all past canoe trips, the hard-shoving, full Río Apure. I placed one foot gingerly on the gunwale, testing the shell for stability much as a swim-mer tests the water for temperature. Chico laughed at this. A small space had been left for me and, entering the canoe, I sat back on my heels with knees down on some loose boards that lay on the moist bottom—a suitably prayerful attitude, it occurred to me, as my finger tips felt water on both sides. My anxiety had little rational basis. I had nine dugout trips already to my credit; during them I had nei-ther witnessed nor experienced a single spill. Someone watching from the steps tossed a pole and a paddle to the man in the bow, then untied the rope and was about to give the boat a shove into the stream when a peremptory voice called from the bank.

We all looked up, and there standing like the ghosts of my airfield interrogators were two soldiers bristling with arms—rifles, cartridge belts, *Wehrmacht* hats and all. I had no idea what was said during the sharp exchange between Chico and the soldiers, but it ended in the soldiers brusquely boarding the dugout and squirming into space that did not exist. Chico, noticing my apprehension, tried by a sympathetic look to convey something, but I did not understand and we were shoved off. The current here close to the wharf was mild and for the first few minutes we drifted, while Chico tugged at the motor's starting cord. With each tug the boat would roll as though to go over. This happened about five times; on the sixth, the motor sputtered uncertainly, then roared into full vigorous life. The dugout, hewn of a tree from Venezuelan highlands, sliced deep and straight into the main current.

Like most things in life, the quality of a river depends on the angle from which it is viewed. Seen from the San Fernando wharf, the Río Apure was a swift, silent expanse heaving eastward, at the same time pushing broad slick palms and narrow slick fingers wherever its banks were too low to resist. Here now from my reverent position and with my eyes not many inches above water level, the river took on an almost firmamental character. The river had ceased being a discrete entity; it and we seemed to melt into one great watery whole. Unseen irregularities of the bottom— thirty to forty feet below us here—drove masses of water upward to create the effect of oil being stirred. There were no white water, no rapids, only heaving bulges and great slow-moving whirls with speedy short-lived central suction holes, and wheeling eddies whose outer edges danced heavily with the outer edges of other eddies. All this moved eastward with the current, eastward where in 100 miles the Apure would wed the Orinoco.

Such llanos channels as the Río Apure derive their volume from a drainage area lying like a barely tilted pancake all the way across Venezuela, through Colombia, to the very foot of the Andes. Six months of precipitation falling on these thousands of square miles has no choice but to be concentrated and crowded into deep surging flood flows which dump their loads into the Orinoco for ultimate exit to the sea.

Soon we passed the airfield of poignant memory; then Chico eased the boat out of the main channel, and we followed a course along the shallower and less ugly waters near the bank. Actually no bank was visible, only a wall of grass higher than a man. Occasionally there would be a break in the wall and I would see surfaces of thick green soup pressing deep into the grillwork of grass.

One of Chico's men had taken a position in the very bow of the craft, where he stood, eyes sharp front, semaphoring now with his right arm, now with his left. I noticed that Chico watched these signals rather than the river or the wall of grass. In so lengthy and low-riding a boat it is difficult for anyone seated in the stern to see what is happening off the bow. The motorman must therefore depend on eyes other than his own for intelligence regarding shallows, submerged logs or muck—trouble ahead of any sort.

Sometimes our guiding line of grass would be replaced by high shrubbery or a stand of plantain or a scarp of trees half or wholly covered with creepers. The farther we got from San Fernando, the heavier the jungle scarp became. Everything in this world—the algal scum on quiet water wherever there was a bank indentation, the lianas stitching other vegetation into one mass, the prairie of grass whenever visible out beyond the riverside tangle—all this shone with a nearly fluorescent quality of green. I had the sense of one passing through a giant hothouse redolent with the gases of leaf transpiration, muggy with humidity, sensuous with warmth. No need for thermostat or hygrometer in this conservatory, for never, day or night, during the llanos winter does temperature escape the 80-85° bracket; and the damp is never much below saturation. Here, a mere 7° north of the equator, my brow was continually moist with unevaporating perspiration. This hothouse even had the equivalent of a paint-dappled glass top for softening the sunlight: the rain clouds clinging low over the wintertime llanos rarely allow the sun to scorch—only to reach a level optimal for profuse botanic growth. The constant warmth, the sodden atmosphere and the softly diffused sunlight— these are ingredients which together produce the nearly incredible verdure of this land.

Not that one need journey to llanos floodlands to witness the miracle of photosynthesis; northern forests and marshes too are green. But the plant life that I observed as our boat moved eastward along the Apure's south bank had a luster seldom seen in temperate climes, a luster far more brilliant than that of the true tropical rain forest where treetop canopies so reduce light penetration that undergrowth usually takes on more somber tones.

The fact that photosynthetic plants comprise the great energy backbone supporting most other forms of life is a commonplace, yet I find it as dramatic a conception as the planet affords. The precise means by which chlorophyll and its associated pigments and enzymes enable plants to bind radiant energy into basic carbohydrate molecules is chemically weird and still constitutes a major mystery. But the process itself, without which animal life and its evolution, as we know it, could never have occurred, goes on tirelessly within the untold trillions of green-laden cells of the plant world. Upon the products of these synthesizing cells, we—all creatures on earth—are in a very real sense dependent. When one says the sun illuminates the world, one says also that the sun gives life to the world. In passing through this green, warm, humid, softly sunlit llanos hothouse I felt very close to the magic wand of all life.

From my canoe position, plants of the creeper, climber and liana variety were the most conspicuous flora of the Apure jungle, covering from my sight a primary and infinitely diversified plant world underneath. In temperate-zone forests the rule tends often to solid stands of single species—pine, oak, beech, etc. But pure uniform cultures are rare in tropical forests. A tree of one species may be abloom with flowers, while its immediate neighbor of another species hangs rich with ripening fruit; the next tree of yet another species may be covered with new green leaves, while a fourth is rusty with leaves ready to drop. All melt together into one solid heterogeneous growth of light- and space-hungry pushers and edgers.

Here, in mid-wet season, the jungle lining the Río Apure, while not so massive and towering as the traditional tropical rain forest where precipitation is more or less continual throughout the year, showed nevertheless a number of rain-forest characteristics. Indeed, common to any jungle, be it in the Amazon valley or along a llanos stream, is a climate gradient extending downward from penthouse to basement. At the very top the world is one of sky, cloud, rain, sun and breeze. Directly under the foliage canopy the light lessens, the air grows still, until in the deep shadows near the jungle floor it is almost entirely without motion and is humid to a point approaching saturation. The basement is choked with rotting remains, with heaps of soft damp humus—or, as in this case, with flood water.

Producing and at the same time occupying this climate gradient is a glorious botanical hodgepodge. There are the plants whose strong supportive structures enable them independently to reach up and draw life from sunlight—the timbered giants whose dense pates form the jungle's upper canopy, then downward through a succession of smaller trees, shrubs, bushes, herbs. Some of these are high and mighty, others are low and fragile, but all rise unaided from the ground.

In contrast are the plants which, despite their gift of photosynthesis, find it a mechanical necessity to lean on others for help—the creepers, climbers and lianas. These do not have sufficiently strong trunk systems independently to support a foliage crown up where the light is strong. They are obliged to twist and coil their cablelike stems upward around the trunks of the jungle's more solid citizens, the while dropping aerial roots, swinging out in looped festoons, sewing, squeezing, weaving and winding—all in order to get their green parts into the zone of photosynthesis where, far from their root sources, they may bask, breathe and blossom.

Another group of plants at home in the jungle, the epiphytes, depend nearly as much on the substantial citizens. Mistletoes, orchids, aerial mosses, lichens and a hundred other such types often eschew all connection with the ground, selecting perch positions wherever space and support can be found, often decorating the jungle's internal framework with bouquets of green and color; some, insinuating root systems into the host's tissues so as to suck out nutrient sap.

No epiphytes were visible to me there within the emerald bank of the Apure; neither momentarily visible were the fungi—the molds, mildews, yeasts, smuts, mushrooms, puffballs, etc. and many of the bacteria, sometimes classified as fungi. Fungi are distinguished from higher plants by their lack of chlorophyll and consequent inability to utilize light energy directly. Then my eyes fell on a plaque of gray "damp-rot" on the wooden gunwale of the dugout no more than three inches from where my right hand rested. And had the skin of that same hand been magnified a few thousand times I should have seen yet another type of fungus—millions and millions of bacterial organisms clinging to my hairs, living in the pores of my sweat glands, minute dots and rods of protoplasm not only on my skin but on and in nearly every object comprising the external world.

Except for the so-called autotrophic bacteria which can metabolize certain inorganic materials, all fungi, to survive, must be parasitic in or on the bodies, carcasses or metabolic products of other plants and animals. That fungus "damp-rot" there on the gunwale was slowly digesting the remains of what was once a green tree, thus to secure life-supporting energy; those bacteria on my skin were deriving sustenance from the exudates of my cutaneous glands or from particles of dead epidermis. And in those vials of penicillin in my first-aid kit hidden somewhere deep in my luggage was a toxic material elaborated, in nature, by a mold species to prevent itself from being overrun by yet lower fungi of the bacteria group.

The Apure mudbank, where visible, extended only six or eight inches above the level of the river. We would occasionally see a hut, although the frequency of human habitation had decreased rapidly as we left San Fernando behind. The sad-looking peon inhabitants of such river abodes would watch solemnly and silently as we passed, or more often we would see only a tired head rising slightly up out of a hammock strung from the stanchions of an open-sided thatched-roof shed. Now with the river at crest, every day was a 24-hour siesta. Human life had run down to a near halt here, and waiting had become the preoccupation— waiting for December and for the waters to recede.

We pulled up along the bank of one such domicile. Our woman with the umbrella and child jumped ashore, together with the girl; then, at a word from Chico, the woman disappeared into the near-by hut. The only sign of the twentieth century here were some large crudely painted numerals on one of the hut's mud-masoned walls. These were a public record of the DDT spraying by a government sanitation crew six months before. Venezuela is in theory very progressive these days, but its progress, at least in these remote parts, has been largely by decree and hence has given rise to some strange anachronisms. A large proportion of llanos peons live in utter and unimaginable filth, with pigs, chickens and dogs competing with children for *lebensraum*. These illiterate peons of the Venezuela back country sense vaguely that something of social importance is astir but have little idea as to what or why. Except for the occasional dry-season visit of an itinerant priest or a pair of soldiers on a fact-finding mission or some government men with sprays, life still proceeds here much as it did a hundred years ago.

The woman had now returned from the hut with a gourd scoop which she gave to Chico. Neither she nor the girl reboarded; they were home, and we were off again. The soldiers had said not a word on the journey so far.

Why Chico wanted an extra bailing scoop was soon evident. Rain had been threatening since San Fernando, and now it began—a gentle drizzle at first, then a deluge, warm, almost hot, splashing on all sides of us and keeping the river surface at a steady boil. That we were in for a spell seemed indicated by the wet-weather look of a horizontal totem pole that suddenly appeared from out of the downpour and passed us not more than twenty feet away, going upstream, San Fernando-ward. By count there were eleven passengers in that dugout, all men, lined up one behind the other. Dark-faced and outwardly sullen, they kept their eyes straight ahead. All were hunched down under voluminous black ponchos. A wintertime llanero, whether in a boat or on a horse, is never without such a garment in which he also sleeps. A man so attired will retain a certain amount of dryness even through the worst of downpours, for the lightly woven fabric acts as an efficient water repellent. His head is, of course, exposed, but not much of it. All those in the dugout had on brow-covering sombreros like the ones worn by Chico and his men. Unmoving and ostensibly unseeing, they slipped by like spirits incarnate. Only the apparition at the motor looked over and waved weakly at Chico.

By this time our own ponchos had been distributed, and

soon we six were converted into similar netherworld heaps of black wool. The soldiers and I kept our heads under our ponchos during the worst phases of the downpour. At intervals the outboard would sputter to a stop, and, while someone held up a blanket shield to prevent water contamination, Chico would refill the fuel tank. Chico's two men took turns bailing, but there was always enough water in the canoe's curved bottom to keep my feet, legs and seat well soaked.

It should be added parenthetically that we were not finding our canoe confinement as physically harassing as conditions would seem to demand. For if not tipsy, we six were by this time a bit euphoric, as is said. It had begun when we left the mudbank after depositing our feminine passengers. Chico, suddenly quick and eager, had extracted from somewhere among his fuel cans a nice clean quart bottle of hard spirits and had begun uncorking it. Here we were on a bulging cresting river, in a boat about as rollproof as a floating pencil and so waterlogged that, if capsized, it would probably have gone down like a length of lead pipe. And how about the caribes and crocodiles? My opinion had always been that the party is safe so long as the driver stays sober. Now I saw our driver take not only a drink but one that seemed about twice as long and thorough as the standard swig, then pass the bottle to the passengers, who did likewise. In the circumstances I could either commend myself to higher powers for mercy, or demand, quite impossibly, being returned to San Fernando. I accepted the first and mandatory alternative.

Drinking (for those llaneros who can afford it) is as characteristic of llanos river travel as rain, heavy loads and swift current. About every half hour during any long journey a bottle, cognac usually, is passed the length of the boat. Everyone has a pull. I had been told, and with time came fully to believe and experience, that this practice serves to stimulate the circulation of those cramped for hours in a dugout's tight quarters and to rosy up the gloom of rain and the everlasting overcast of the wet season. Nor is this explanation an idle excuse, for alcohol is known to increase cutaneous blood flow and to induce a slight lowering of internal body temperature, the latter effect being of considerable value in these hot climes. As to the dangerous side, one of the prerequisites of a good river pilot seems to be that he be able to hold his liquor. Never once during my Apure travels did I see a motorman, even after he'd had innumerable swigs, exhibit any overt signs of intoxication; nor did I ever see drunken behavior on the part of canoe-confined passengers.

A half hour after our arrival at Arichuna I was being served supper in a native hut. There being no visible facilities for washing the day's accumulation of grime off my hands and face, I had immediately sat down at the only table in the hut. The floor on which my bare feet rested was hard-caked sod, and the entree was a beef stew of sorts. A kerosene light hanging from a crossbeam low under the peaked thatched roof shone on a circle of what I shall call my admirers. No longer were the two soldiers brusque and formal. The cognac had no doubt contributed to this miracle, although I prefer to think that we Apure comrades, even without the liquor, would have found common ground for nonverbal understanding during that long afternoon in the canoe. Whatever its basis, the amiability of our rapport was indicated by the action on the part of one of the soldiers who, as we stepped out of the dugout that night, had come over like a rain-soaked munitions dump and patted my shoulder affectionately, pointing to himself and saying, "Juan."

Eagerly accepting the law's proffered cordiality, I designated myself as "Pablo," a disclosure that pleased Juan very much, and he shoulder-patted me with great feeling. My face was looking down over his shoulder into the muzzle of his rifle. I was not quite sure but that this sudden friendship had something in common with the sort of warm but brief entente a deputy and his prisoner must experience on their trip from the Tombs to Ossining.

I was a little embarrassed by the way my companions appeared to be lionizing me. I sat at the small rustic table like an Apure potentate, while the members of my council, working on their bowls of stew and cups of coffee, sat on boxes or on the ground. But each seemed more intent on my bowl and cup than on his own, alert to call the cook-shed in my behalf whenever one or the other needed refilling. There were no pensions or restaurants in Arichuna. This hut was the home of a local widow who could be solicited into serving a meal to stray travelers. Chico had led me here after we deposited our hammock bundles in a large hut elsewhere in the village, the public sala where river travelers like us could put up for the night. Arichuna was a village en route between San Fernando and Chico's ranch; we would continue our journey in the morning.

The meal was about over when into the hut from out of the darkness stepped a young man who, despite his llanos apparel, appeared to be of Anglo-European origin. He had been told of the arrival of a foreigner—a unique development in Arichuna—and had come to investigate. He tried to speak to me in Spanish, but, getting nowhere, he turned to Chico, from whom he quickly got some sort of explanation of my presence. The newcomer, a tall and gaunt man with steady eyes, turned to me again and, somewhat irrelevantly, I thought, said, *"Parla Lei italiano?"*

"No," I had to reply.

"Parlez-vous français?"

"Muy poco," I replied.

"Sprechen sie Deutsch?" he persisted, unimpressed with my Spanish promise of French.

"Sí," I replied with enthusiasm, quickly adding, *"Ja-wohl."*

With this, his face brightened, and his conversation immediately shifted into precise and beautifully spoken German. To me it seemed as though a breath of fresh air had entered my language prison, for, although my German wasn't fluent, I could speak it reasonably well and could understand it easily. I quietly thanked God for this Germanic version of Siso, for German he was. I soon learned that he, Dr. Blecker, had been in the medical department of the German Army during World War II. After the war, which he called a *"Schlacht,"* he had emigrated to Venezuela and on to the interior in his desire to get as far away from organized civilization as possible. He had gladly accepted an appointment as government *médico* for this Arichuna district, so remote and primitive that few self-respecting Venezuelan physicians would think of taking it.

This talk was music to my ears, for not only had I found someone with whom for the first time in weeks I could converse on a more meaningful level than with Siso, but there was a community of interests in medical matters; for, as I have said, when red birds do not compete biological and medical research is my profession. Furthermore, Dr.

Blecker seemed personally a sympathetic soul, interested in natural history too, and did not consider my bird search as something to be smiled about. The session ended with an insistence that I revise my sleeping plans for the night. My newly found friend was living the life of a bachelor and was hungry for conversation with an outsider, especially an American. There could be no question: I must come to his quarters. Chico did not seem displeased about this, so I bade him good night with the understanding that we would meet in the morning. *El médico* and I stepped out into the now rainless Arichuna night.

Situated in the midst of this village of either straw-, tile- or tin-roofed dwellings, Dr. Blecker's living quarters had a floor of solid concrete. This type of floor construction was designed to keep out overt water, which it did well enough; but it did not prevent a heavy ground moisture from seeping through. The quarters, consisting of two rooms, consequently had an atmosphere of heavy dankness, like all four-walled buildings in the llanos in wintertime, and the meager wooden furnishings were fertile with varieties of fungus. Combine these circumstances with a 24-hour day unchangingly in the 80s and one has a reason why, perennially, so many a temperate-zoner has avoided the tropics as a place of permanent abode.

But there are means available these days for making such conditions less oppressive. The heart of Dr. Blecker's sitting room was a full-sized kerosene refrigerator. First thing he did after entering the room and turning on a mantel lamp was to open the refrigerator and draw out two bottles of carbonated fruit beverage. With a swallow of this ice-cold elixir, the dampness and heat of the atmosphere vanished and life seemed to smile. Nor was it the fruit drink per se; it could just as well have been iced milk, beer, water, or a highball. The kerosene refrigerator is a sesame to proper living in the unelectrified tropics; air-conditioning, when technically and economically feasible, will complete the job.

Another point of view, often stated, is that modern sanitation and medicine are the great hope of the tropics. Clean out malaria, control the parasites, yellow fever, typhoid, yaws, the venereal diseases—and the vast pool of drowsing humanity inhabiting the planet's equatorial belt will awaken. I had always subscribed to this view and was therefore interested later in the evening to get a dissenting or at least qualified opinion from one well able to speak.

There was, of course, no bathroom in Dr. Blecker's rooms; I washed up in a basin of water resting on a corner stand. The toilet, out in back of the house, was, as in my San Fernando hotel, a cement hole. I visited it with a flashlight and noticed something at the bottom of the hole which all but canceled the effect of the cold drink. There, half embedded in the feculent accumulation, sat three toads so enormous as to be unable, or perhaps unwilling, to escape the hole which they had obviously entered earlier in their lifetimes. They looked up at the light, waiting, it seemed, for their next meal of human droppings; they presented, along with the flies buzzing around them, a picture so loathsome as to be unmentionable except perhaps, as in the following instance, among biologists.

"I would bet that if I dissected one of those toads," I commented upon my return to the room where we had been sitting in our hammocks, "I could find samples of every parasite in the books."

This opinion no doubt carried elements of exaggeration, but Blecker threw up his hands in despairing agreement. In German, not halting like my own, he began a rambling discourse. "I am supposed to practice medicine here." He was pointing at, then got up and went over to, a huge shipping carton which he opened for my benefit. "The government medical-supply office in Caracas sends me all these expensive pharmaceuticals." He picked up a handful of small boxes and vials, which I saw contained penicillin, vitamins, hormone preparations, etc. "All useful," he commented, "but there is only one type without which I could not get along—the antihelminthics, the antimalarials, in short the antiparasite drugs. I am responsible for the health of the people in this Arichuna district. They pay no money; the bill is paid by foreigners who buy Venezuelan oil. Tomorrow morning you will visit my office. There you will see the peons waiting. A quick examination to rule out any acute condition, then I prescribe a worm purge. I tell them to come back if that does not cure, and I will look for other causes. Often they fail to come back. But if they do and I prescribe another medicine, they carry it home, perhaps take one dose. If no effects are felt almost within minutes, they are likely to throw the bottle away. It may happen that I will not see them again until they are half dead, and then it is the priest who calls me, not their family."

"The old story, I suppose."

"Yes, without doubt." Blecker continued. "The teacher should always come before the physician, is that not so? Human beings must have knowledge before they can benefit much from medical advice. Ninety per cent of the diseases here could be prevented by basic elementary education. If the peons could but read simple instructions, could but understand the rudiments of sanitation! These parasites, this half-cooked beef and pork that they eat . . ." I recalled a quotation from Bolívar that I had seen conspicuously inscribed above the door of a school in San Fernando, in substance: LEARNING IS THE FIRST NECESSITY OF OUR PEOPLE.

Our discussion of parasitism began to range away from peon patients, away from privy toads. Blecker, as a practicing physician, necessarily viewed parasitism as the exploitation of the human body by a lower organism thus to produce either a specific disease or at least a state of debility. But he was aware that this was a somewhat limited view and seemed to welcome a give-and-take on the broader aspects of the subject.

In the world of free nature the parasite is not to be considered primarily a disease producer, but rather an organism adapting its life to an easy source of food or to an environment of convenient shelter. Nor by any means are all parasites harmful. The millions of bacteria and yeast cells that grow in the human mouth and there derive nutrient from the salivary fluids neither contribute to nor harm the host; the myriad microorganisms, flora and fauna, that live in the lower intestinal tracts of most animals are likewise innocuous. The remora fish, to cite in this regard a creature of the visible world, clings by means of special suckers to the side of a shark or turtle, traveling far and wide as a hitchhiker, releasing its hold only long enough to eat the crumbs that fall from the master's table; and there are the sedentary hydroid animals that attach themselves innocently to seaweed, and those epiphytic plants that live without detriment to their hosts on the branches of trees. In context with the privy-toad subject that had got us off on this tack in the first place, there is a species of fish that chooses a reclusive life in the rectum of the sea cucumber, without apparent discomfort or harm to the latter. Commensalism is the term applied when, as in the foregoing examples, one member of the association derives specific benefit but not at the cost of damage to the other.

Symbiosis, a second type of harmless parasitism found widely spread in nature, differs from commensalism in that *both* organisms derive gain from their relationship. Termites, for example, could not benefit from the wood they eat if it were not for the flagellate protozoa that inhabit their intestinal tracts. The termite supplies raw material and shelter in return for which the protozoa convert cellulose into a form digestible to the termite host; separate these partners, and they starve; keep them together, and they thrive. The biological world is full of symbiotic relationships: ants that protect and feed aphid "cows" in exchange for honeydew "milk"; birds that are permitted to pick food remains from the teeth of crocodiles or vermin from the hides of water buffalo and rhinos, in return, apparently, for their automatic function as aerial lookouts; luminous bacteria that supply light for the photophores of deep-sea fish in return for sustenance and shelter.

The parasites of pathology, parasites which exploit and injure, include those that produce disease in animals and plants, as well as in human beings. Here the technique of "boring from within" has been developed to formidable lengths. Once having learned, during evolution, how to gain entrance to the nutritionally rich environment of another's body, such a parasitizing organism, unless restrained by immunological or other defense reactions within the victim's body or by applied therapy, multiplies, often with wild explosiveness, to overwhelm the helpless host by means of metabolic poisons or by direct interference with organic function. The biological meaning of such killing action on the part of an invading parasite is obscure, for with the downfall of the food-supplying host the invader too must die or pass on to another host. It is unthinkable that such organisms have any specific intention of killing their hosts, thus to destroy a rich food source and, incidentally, themselves. Whether parasites kill because of a headlong urge and opportunity to multiply, or because of the absence of defensive restraints on the part of the victim, is a classical question both in ecology and pathology.

More transparently sensible would seem to be the action of those parasite species that invade a foreign organism, there to prosper and multiply without overrunning or, so to speak, killing the goose that lays the golden egg. A great variety of parasites quietly inhabit the intestines, skin, liver, kidneys, lungs, blood stream, muscles, etc., of most animals in the wild state, there to wallow in nutrient-bearing fluids, while proliferating or becoming encysted—all without inflicting immediate damage to the host. The jungle tiger may appear sleek and magnificent and may roar and exhibit his fangs as though he were lord of the universe. But finding shelter in his pelage and sipping his blood are mites and fleas; inhabiting his digestive tract are millions of parasitic protozoa and bacteria; and tunneling through his vital tissues are worms, flukes and flagellates—there attaining a kind of refuge from the competitive strain of the world outside. Perhaps their having found this security is what causes internal parasites often to become structurally so degenerate as to lose all functions other than those involving food absorption and reproduction—but they do survive and, if only in a reproductive sense, they flourish, drifting rather than swimming in the stream of life. Poetic justice may be said to prevail in many of these cases: parasites too have parasites; "fleas have lesser fleas"; even protozoa may harbor symbionts and parasites; while bacteria are never free from the threat of bacteriophages. The world of crashing antlers and ripping talons is only one aspect of the struggle for existence.

How parasitism arose in evolution is difficult if not impossible to tell, mainly because of the bewildering diversity of life cycles found among parasitic organisms and also because of the broad scope within which parasitism asserts itself. Consider the notorious protozoan that spends one portion of its life in the body of an anopheles mosquito, another in the blood stream of a man; the bilharzial fluke which uses a snail as an intermediate host, prior to infecting man; the sleeping-sickness trypanosome transmitted by the tsetse fly. Every organism is impelled to adapt itself to shelter and a food source, or a combination of these, suitable to its specific metabolic and reproductive needs—be it a woodland stream or a blood stream, a grass-covered field or a hair-covered hide, a cesspool or a rectum. It is perhaps not unlikely that most cases of parasitism arose in evolution first as shelter associations, then gradually becoming commensal, then symbiotic, and finally one-sidedly parasitic. Parasitic exploitation has existed almost as far back as the record goes. Insect galls have been found in Cretaceous fossils 100 million years old; parasitic sea snails in Silurian fossils 400 million years old. The remains of bilharzial infection have been observed in the kidneys of Egyptian mummies.

Blecker refilled my glass with some more of that wonderful cold drink from his refrigerator. Through the screened door of the house I saw small weak stars in the sky—the first I had seen since my arrival in the llanos. Drinks in hand, we rose and went out for a bit into the night, and sauntered down a short way to the edge of the high, silent Apure whose expanse was saved from black invisibility by that dim astronomical glimmer far above. I was glad to be off that river, if only temporarily. Tonight it seemed too placid for a thing so powerful; the air seemed not to have changed a whit from its tepid humidity-laden daytime character; the going underfoot seemed more slushy, if anything. Occasionally the sharp yapping of a dog or the slap of Blecker's or my hand against an unseen mosquito would break into the melancholy quiet of the sleeping village. Now and then the figure of a man or boy or woman, silhouetted darkly against the river's vague sheen, would appear on the path which ran along the water's edge. Like a wraith, the figure would melt into the blackness as softly as it had come.

Blecker had told me earlier of having been seriously wounded in the war. "In Europe," he was saying, "as, I suppose, in America, the sulfa drugs and the antibiotics have reduced bacterial disease to near the zero point. Yes," he continued, apparently reflecting on his wartime experience, "in Europe the body is well, the soul is sick. Here the body is sick, the soul . . ." He hesitated and laughed, not bothering to finish the sentence or to define his use of the word *soul.*

Perhaps Dr. Blecker was inviting my opinion on the spiritual condition of man. But since this is a subject that must be charily approached, even between the best of friends, I let it drop there. However, I could not avoid the private reflection that thoughtful men these days, perhaps more than ever before, are concerned with the meaning of spirit in a materialistic world. Some sense, some profess to know, that a man is more than the mere gene carrier for his species; but who can prove it, who can articulate it? Our physiologists, psychologists and psychiatrists have done so thorough a job that a prophet who, keeping within the context of modern science, could demonstrate that the human individual is something more than a biochemical system reacting to its environment might well find the world at mid-twentieth century a fertile field.

It was not a conversational impasse but mosquitoes that drove us back before long behind the barrier of the screen door, back to the living room with the refrigerator, where we settled again a bit sleepily on our hammocks. Blecker was telling me about a small farm he had been able to buy a few miles inland from the river. Already he had thirty head of cattle. If I did not mind some mud wading, I must come out and see the ranch; there was a lagoon there too, and many water birds. By this time I had, of course, told Blecker of my scarlet-ibis aims and of my disappointments so far. He knew of Chico's garcero and believed that I would probably find every bird species of the llanos represented there. "And when you are through with Chico, you must return here and stay with me for a few days. Only with my friend Don Carlos, in San Fernando, do I occasionally have the opportunity to talk as we have been doing tonight."

I was genuinely pleased to accept his invitation. My host got up to turn off the gasoline lantern, preparatory to turning in. I thought I would like to clear up one additional matter. "Tell me, *Herr Doktor,* do you have any idea why those soldiers were sent to accompany me?"

"Who can tell?" he replied. "Soldiers often come down-river from San Fernando on missions of one sort or another. Always in this country the party in power controls the *Guardia Nacional.* Those out of power sometimes seek to undermine it. Perhaps the authorities think you are an agent who must be watched." He laughed. There was a pause; then, as in a movie double-take, he added, "You are not, are you?"

"Confidentially, I am. I seek evidence of red activity in the state of Apure."

There were no more words. My attempt at humor had misfired badly.

Late the next afternoon the original San Fernando six arrived at Chico's place. Like so many of the other llanos ranch houses I had seen, this one stood on a bank not more than a foot above flood level. It was no peon's hut, nor was it a palace. Yet the main dwelling, thatch-roofed like the others, was large enough to establish Chico as one of the more prosperous llaneros of the area. Here the word *prosperous* is highly relative: Chico had no electricity, no ice-box, no beds, no plumbing, no cement floor, no anything that made home life for him any different than it had been for his great-great-grandfather. He had a sizable herd of cattle, but except for a few milk cows out back of the hut cluster the cattle would not be seen until the waters receded and the roundup began. Chico, like all these river dwellers, ate, drank, slept and idled during the wet season; there was no alternative. During the dry season it would be different; then all able-bodied men would take to horse and round up the cattle and herd them great distances to market centers. Sometimes roundup time came and, if the Apure had risen too high that season, there would be no cattle to be found—only bloated carcasses covered with mud or chewed on by the tigers.

There was something pixyish about Chico. After his womenfolk had served coffee to me and the soldiers, he began poking around the crate containing my new and untried outboard. He could see that the motor was a model quite different from any used hereabouts; the remote fuel tank and the reverse gear of this latest American model were magic to him, and before very long he caught my eye and pointed to a dugout tied in the water next to the one we had used for the trip from San Fernando, but only a third the latter's size. Then he pointed to the motor crate, indicating the desirability of a demonstration. By a skillful use of sign language, Chico made it plain that the small boat was to be mine for the duration of my visit and that in it I would be able to come and go as I chose; the garcero was a half-hour river trip from the ranch house. Before it gets dark, Chico was trying to say, let's see if the small canoe will be suitable for use with your motor.

This suggestion did not sit too well with me. In the first place, we had been drinking cognac again that day. In the second place, the river here was as treacherous as I had seen it anywhere. In the third place (and this is an admission that surprises even myself), I had never in my life operated an outboard. I had observed them in use many times, at home on fishing trips with other people running the motor; I had carefully studied the literature received when I bought the motor; but as to actually operating one,

I was literally inexperienced. In laying plans for the scarlet-
ibis expedition I had always had in mind using the motor
on some sort of tipproof skiff, dory or dinghy. With such
a boat there would be no danger, and I would be able to
practice in safety. Moreover, in bringing the motor along
with me to Chico's place, I had planned to hire one of his
men to be my motorman and pilot.

Here now suddenly, in a land where basic manhood and
social respectability are to a considerable extent appraised
on boating skill or, in summer, on horsemanship, I was on
the spot. To have turned to Chico and said, "Here's the
motor; you attach it to the canoe and try it out" would
have been a sign of bloodlessness, and as an admitted ten-
derfoot my stock would quickly have tottered.

If I could only have been alone for a while, to have
experimented close to shore and tried the motor at very
slow speeds at first! I sensed well enough what Chico expected: I would be no man's man if I didn't know how to
handle this motor, if I couldn't prove it by zipping out into
the stream and putting on a virtual aquacade. And this
must be done in full view of spectators entirely sophisti-
cated regarding such matters.

Surely without the afternoon's cognac to reinforce my
character I would have yielded to good judgment and
then and there demurred—thus, of course, jeopardizing
Chico's good will and the aid I needed in locating the
coro-coros next day. No, this was clearly not the time for
conservative good judgment. I suddenly stood up boldly
and, as though knowing exactly what I was up to, proceeded to unpack the motor. Soon it lay on the grass, shiny
as a new pin, as complex to me as the detonating mechanism of an atom bomb. There was the extra propeller that

Billy Phelps had advised me to bring along; there were the two dozen shear pins, the extra spark plugs, the extra gaskets, the tool kit; there were the bright-red newfangled fuel tank and the rubber tubing still in their factory wrappings.

A good angel helped me lift the heavy monster and carry it to the water's edge. Chico was watching with intense interest, as were the soldiers, several farm hands and a gathering of dogs and children. Not only is this fellow a famous *norteamericano*, they were thinking, but he is an expert with outboard motors; we will learn something from him. See the sure skill with which he carries the motor. Under the grass eaves of the house I saw the womenfolk attentive too.

Then rushing out of heaven to support me as I stepped into the tiny dugout again came divine help. The god in charge of gravity was a little late in arriving, and I and the boat underwent a dangerous rolling lurch, almost spilling all into the caribe-suspect water. But that spirit arrived just in the split second of time necessary to correct the unbalance. I walked down the length of the canoe, carrying my motor with the ostensible assurance of a tightrope walker with his balance pole. Then I lowered the clamp side of the motor down onto the stern plate and turned the screws tight. I could hear the "ah's" of admiration over the ease with which this maneuver was being executed. Willing hands were now handing me the fuel tank, which we had previously filled with three gallons of oil-gasoline mix; then the tubing.

Once more divine powers came to my rescue, this time by holding a mental image of the instruction-book diagram before my eyes. No one on the bank noticed how I studied that mental picture; all they saw was how I calmly affixed the tubing ends to their proper places, pumped pressure into the fuel tank, primed the motor and began tugging at the starting cord. Again my mind's eye was on the diagram in that instruction booklet, and my fingers were advised to turn various knobs, to adjust various levers. There was a little more cord pulling.

Suddenly the motor gave out with some brief sputters, then broke into the happy music of a gentle purr. Because their outboards had no neutral gear position, these llanos people were accustomed to shoving their canoes out into the stream before starting to pull the cord. Indeed, there had been some apprehensive calling from the group as I took the end of the cord in hand; and an effort had been made to untie the line securing the canoe to a shore sapling. Here now, great wonder, the motor was going—but not the boat! A murmur of admiration seemed to swell from the openmouthed crowd. I raced the motor a couple of times, turned it off, and then smiled and gesticulated to Chico the following wordless message: "Well, you see it actually runs, and quite well, too. Now let's go inspect your farm. How about showing me your milk cows?"

But alas, the nonverbal method of communication here proved inadequate. Chico hopped into the canoe with me and signaled the soldiers and a couple of the men to do likewise. In a second the boat's gunwales were near the water line. Please, a demonstration ride upriver, señor.

As events unfolded, there would not even have been time for me to escape shoreward, for someone had already untied the boat and shoved it into the stream. Twice, as the men sought sitting positions or jostled or laughed, the craft almost went over. Yes, there was laughter, but not from

Horatio at the controls. I yanked the cord and, an event unparalleled in outboard history, the motor started on the first pull. I crouched down, pushing my power plant into forward gear just as the directions had read, at the same time advancing the throttle. Out into the channel we roared, where a second later the current seized the tiny craft and started sweeping it downriver. By virtue of an undoubted miracle, I suddenly got the feel of the boat and the feel of the rudder tension. Keeping the canoe in balance, I swerved through the current and aligned the bow upstream. Thus, having evaded the first awful danger, I attempted to slow down but apparently pushed something, obviously the accelerator lever, in the wrong direction. Full powerful speed ahead now, and my passengers were confounded by my audaciousness.

With what to everyone but myself seemed like great prowess, I made a sweeping arc in the wide river (I couldn't make a smaller turn, for we were going too fast) and headed back toward shore. How it happened I will never know, but my approach to the bank where the big canoe lay—an approach which, in view of the Apure's current, had earlier in the afternoon been difficult even for Chico—was a masterpiece of piloting. There was no bump, no premature stalling of the motor, only perfection.

My passengers stepped onto the mudbank a bit dazed, overwhelmingly impressed with my motor, worshipful of my skill. I stepped onto the bank with the feeling of one who has just been in close contact with a heavenly hand.

Chapter 3

By SEVEN next morning we were back on the Apure, garcero-bound. In view of the triumph of the evening before, my motor and the small canoe were elected to transport the expedition. Chico was along, of course, to serve as guide and mastermind; two of his peons added their ballast as polesmen, for much of the trip would be across flooded marshes. The insistence of the two military men to come along bothered me a little. However, the fact that their enthusiasm for travel had as much to do with Chico's bottle as with any suspicion of me was substantiated when, hardly five minutes en route, my host and passengers began passing the cognac. The soldiers immediately lost their prison-guard look; in the interests of survival I, at the tiller, abstained.

Clearly we were approaching a dense bird concentration. Everywhere the shallows beyond the river channel were dotted with waders, preponderantly egrets in pure snowy dress, some of them behaving like drunken tap dancers, their wings spread and a-tremble. Watching one, you would see the scissor beak go zipping into the water, aimed at some frog or fish or crustacean. The eater would lift its head in recognition of our approach, but rarely fly off.

About a half mile upriver, Chico indicated that I turn shoreward and cut the motor. From here on we would pole. As we coasted toward the grass, I was aware of a two-way traffic lane of anhingas, no more than thirty feet above my head, beating straight and fast courses either northward or south. Almost all those heading north over the marsh had tufts of grass or sprays of twigs in their beaks. There was no doubt as to the direction in which the garcero lay.

Anhingas are called "snakebirds" in our Gulf states, because they often swim with body submerged and with head and neck extending serpent-like above the surface. They are also called "water turkeys," because when observed in high flight, their tails fanned, there is some resemblance to wild turkeys. That morning on the Río Apure the former was the more appropriate name, for the water seemed full of "snakes." Where one would disappear in a dive, another serpentine head would silently break through the surface and look around. These creatures are magnificent under-water-pursuit swimmers, and woe to any fish that gets within lunge distance of that stiletto beak. Nor do they plunge down out of the sky upon their quarry in the manner of some fish-eating birds; submerged, they swiftly over-take and spear or seize their prey. Their take-off from the water, I noticed that morning, was not especially grace-ful, requiring long splashy surface runs. Some crawled directly out of the water onto logs or bog heaps along the shore shallows.

I had pulled the motor's prop end up out of danger of weed entanglements. The silent brown-faced peon at the bow, leaving his pole as yet untouched in the bottom of the canoe, seized handful after handful of the reedlike grass and pulled us in; a tent of green closed on both sides and partly above. We proceeded, creating a tunnel through the grass, making slow but steady progress, when an incident occurred which reminded me of a jungle scene in a

Grade B movie. The grass, for the moment, had parted a little, and ahead, alongside the narrow channel, stood an ugly tree. One of the tree's nude branches, no more than five feet above head level, extended directly over our course. The bow of the canoe was nearly there when down off the branch flopped the head and fore part of an enormous snake. The thing hung poised in what was a gesture either of threat or fright, mouth gaping a little and eyes evil beyond saying. Our man at the bow, who had been using his pole ever since we left the tall grass, was able by an abrupt lunge to divert the boat from passing directly under the contaminated branch. Chico grabbed a heavy paddle and, as we passed, swung at the head and missed, striking the branch instead. The snake recoiled and in a second had slithered down the tree into an oblivion of water and green.

"He that feareth every bush must never go a-birding" is a sixteenth-century proverb that certainly did not occur to me at the time, but well it might have. The encounter was so unexpected and electrifying that my memory of it is more emotional than factual. Like the witness in court who cannot recall a single feature of his assailant, I cannot say whether that snake was spotted, striped, colored or monotoned. There was a flickering tongue, I think, but whether the horror was an air- or a fire-breather I cannot in truth testify. I will go so far as to speculate, however, that, in view of its unquestioned size, the snake did not belong to any of the venomous species. I will guess further that he belonged to the Boidae, a family of snakes well represented in the South American tropics. To place him in the Boidae is to say that he was either a boa or a python; but we must rule out the latter, for pythons are limited in range to tropical regions of the Old World. So he must have been a boa, which, however, is not to say that he was a boa constrictor, for that appellation, in correct herpetological nomenclature, is reserved for a single species named, with literal conciseness, *Constrictor constrictor*. Yet, if he belonged to the Boidae, then he certainly practiced constriction, for all members of this family kill their prey by coiling and squeezing. Actually, it takes a well-trained specialist to differentiate the two subfamilies, Boinae and Pythoninae, for members of the latter differ from those of the former only in the possession of a supraorbital skull bone. To make a final rash guess, the creature, as a Boinae, could well have been a medium-sized specimen of anaconda (*Eurectes murinus*), which is where I will abandon my speculation into snake taxonomics.

There was laughter as we passed under the now deserted branch. Juan's reaction time was far slower than the snake's; Juan, with his revolver unholstered, had the pain of frustration on his face as he sought the missing target. No trace of the snake was to be seen—fortunately, for a gunshot would have sent every bird between here and the Orinoco into wild flight. There was more laughter over Juan's disappointment. Although the snake had obviously been a nonvenomous species and was probably more afraid of us than we of it, I confess to being relieved when a little later our canoe emerged from this world of grass and hidden things onto a more or less open lagoon.

It had begun to rain. And this time I was really vexed at the weather, for there through the downpour I could barely make out, as the first sign of the garcero, a line of firm shrubbery backed by a stand of high half-skeletonized trees. In them, standing gloomily in the rain or sitting on close-piled nests, were countless vague spectral shapes.

Egrets, ordinarily puffs of white-white, were now, viewed through a curtain of fast-driving rain, ashen.

But my anxiety over the rain was short-lived, for the downpour ended abruptly and the sun came out to reveal, all of a sudden, what the rain had veiled. The high bare-branched trees were no longer sepulchral; those birds were no longer ashen. Then the still life became animated. Birds —thousands and tens of thousands—began coming and going, fluttering and soaring and perching and brooding, all in one brilliance of incredible profusion. Literally as far as I could see were the darting, flickering, changing shapes of birds—white, blue-gray and black. Perhaps even more remarkable than the visual was the auditory trans-formation. During our approach, the birds had been quiet or perhaps their noises had been masked by the rain. Now I was sensitive to a muted roar, the sound of a big bird city. And with this came some comprehension of the garcero's magnitude.

On the marsh's lower vegetation were mostly egrets— American egrets with white plumage, yellow bills and black feet; snowy egrets with white plumage, black bills and yellow feet—in a panorama suggestive of a field of pod-bursting cotton. The high trees, most clearly seen from our present position, were full of occupied anhinga nests. Every branch crotch was piled deep with a nest; every little twig cluster was loaded. So dense was the dis-tribution of nests that one could hardly see through the trees into the sky beyond. The anhingas were in all stages of activity: in those nests where the head and beak of a brooding parent appeared there must have been eggs; where the adult was sitting attentively on the edge of the nest or on a near-by branch there were certainly young.

The male anhingas could easily be distinguished from the females, even at a distance, because of their characteristic gray back feathers. The air above the trees was like that over a swarming beehive. Our canoe was lost in the great dimensions of the garcero, and the birds seemed scarcely aware of our intrusion.

There was no land anywhere, and it was quite evident that our searching would have to be accomplished wholly from the canoe, which at this point had come up to a solid foliage bank ornamented with the brooding, plume-bearing egrets and rendered the more lovely in the sun by an entanglement of morning-glory vines and their blue blossoms. As we proceeded in close parallel with the foliage bank, the birds at our point of near contact left their nests, exposing eggs and nestlings, many within arm's reach. It occurred to me that a plume hunter with a shotgun could from this single spot have bagged at least a hundred prime egrets.

At length our canoe turned and pierced head on into this thicket. Mosquitoes and flies disturbed from their underleaf positions descended on us unmercifully. Above through the foliage were interminable flashes of sun being reflected from white—egrets hovering, coming, fleeing. I heard a heavy splash in the water somewhere to one side. Chico said "caiman" as casually as you'd say "nice day." This shrubbery we were passing through was not clean and pliable like the grass farther back, but thorned and heavy, and filthy with moist droppings. The air had a hencoop odor. Each of the polesmen had a machete in hand, hacking through wherever the canoe seemed to reach an impasse. But this difficult tunneling did not last long, and we came out onto a second open lagoon an acre or two in area. The lagoon had no shores; its limits were wading trees to the north, wading shrubs and smaller trees on both sides, and high, half-swimming water grass to the south, all margined by green scum. The center of the lagoon was sky-blue and beautiful—hiding the menace of caribes, caimans, crocodiles, water snakes. . . . Our polesmen rested for a bit; and, as we looked around, taking it in, even Chico seemed impressed by the great number of birds. It was his first visit to the garcero this season.

I saw a reddish-brown Cebus monkey in the branches of one of the anhinga trees. He was having a field day. When I first spotted him he was absorbed in tearing an anhinga nest to bits. The adult bird owner was up the branch only a foot or two away, completely bewildered by this deliberate destruction of her home, although other anhingas in nests within liberal reach of the monkey seemed unconcerned. The victim bird could have blinded the marauder in two seconds, but apparently she understood the lethal potential of her beak weapon only when underwater in pursuit of fish. She just sat there glowering, with her wings half open. I cannot say for a certainty whether the monkey was actually eating the eggs or just toying with them. Then he began in earnest to tear up the nest, wrecking it beyond all salvation. At this point the harassed parent flew off.

I was suddenly aware that trigger-happy Juan had again got hold of his revolver and was this time taking aim, with some justification I will agree, at the heathen monkey. Even if I had wanted to, it was too late for me to stop him. The report was deafening; the canoe was almost tipped over by our sudden moves; the sky quickly became overcast with a fog of 25,000 flying birds; the hum of the garcero grew into a long, low peal of thunder; and the Cebus primate, missed by a mile, made a fast getaway.

My eyes, intent for scarlet, were on the swirling clouds of screaming birds above: snowy egrets, American egrets, little blue and great blue herons, anhingas, boat-billed night herons, white ibis, now and then a roseate spoonbill. In probably less than two minutes the whole vast birdage had settled and the garcero was back to normal. Concerned over my failure to have seen even so much as a trace of scarlet, I looked at Chico, then, in my handbook Spanish, asked, *"Donde están los coro-coros?"*

He did not answer, but spoke instead to the polesman in the bow, giving instructions of some sort. Then he looked at me and pointed into the distance, indicating, I presumed, that the coro-coros were down at the other end of the garcero, yet to be explored. But something else was pressing on his mind, for he motioned that I watch what he was about to do.

I hadn't noticed until now that between Chico's feet on the bottom of the canoe were two young egrets that he had obviously snatched off a nest as we passed under the egret shrubbery. Now he had one in hand. Its clumsy body, sparsely seeded with white down, looked green because of the color of the underskin. Chico was talking at a great rate, mainly to the soldiers. All were laughing and joking as Chico suddenly tossed his unhappy-looking baby egret into the lagoon. It landed in the water about ten feet from the canoe. All eyes watched it, expectant. But nothing seemed to be happening. The egret floated, kicking its feet in ungainly swimming motion and flapping its stubby wings. There was more joking by all except Chico, who seemed angered.

He grabbed the remaining egret, viciously seized one leg in each hand and jerked. The bird died instantly as a leg was severed from the body, now oozing blood and entrails. Savagely Chico threw these two pieces of bird flesh over close to where the live bird was still floundering.

Then it happened, and Chico let out a roar of delight. The soldiers watched like spectators at a bullfight as the caribes rose to the taste and smell of fresh blood in the water. Within seconds the two fragments of egret were gone. Then the caribe pack, inflamed by the presence of spilled protein in the water, discovered the live bird and it too underwent sudden splashy annihilation.

I could not get a good look at the caribes themselves. Living close to the bottom of such a lagoon, they have the habit of darting up to the surface at any sign of fresh meat, each violently excising a mouthful, then down again. When this attack maneuver is executed simultaneously by great schools of caribes, even so large an animal as a horse has been described as disappearing within minutes. All I saw was a series of streaks in the water, some side-body flashes, a little surface turbulence, and it was over and still.

Later in my llanos travels I had occasion to examine netted caribes up close. Most of those I saw were eight or ten inches long, but I have been told that they often grow to be considerably longer. It is the small devils that are apparently the most dangerous, for it is they that seem to operate most effectively in packs. Out of water the caribe doesn't look especially blood-chilling—just a little fish with bright beady eyes and a pink-red chin and underside. But its nervous system gives it the most aggressively vicious temperament to be found, allegedly, in any fish, perhaps in any animal species. It knows no fear and will attack anything of any size so long as there is a smell of fresh meat about it. Combine this temperament with superb dental armament and you have—well, you have a caribe. Those teeth comprise two arcs of enamel triangle points which, when the jaws snap shut, shear one against the other. The bite is so swift, clean and deep that no ragged edges remain around the area gouged. Freshly spilled blood or open flesh are sure triggers for setting off the attack response.

Caribes (Genus *Serrasalmus,* and varying in species according to the locality in which they are found) are distributed throughout the Amazon basin northward to inland waters over the whole of northern South America. There are few native settlements in this vast area that do not have one or more persons with toes or fingers missing in mute evidence of encounters with caribes. How other aquatic creatures sharing the caribe habitat escape is an interesting question. The answer may involve body exudates that the caribe finds unattractive.

The concentration of such predators in garcero waters has its genesis in those foul nitrogenous droppings. This bird excrement, among the richest of natural fertilizers, converts warm lagoon waters into a culture medium for microorganisms, which comprise the first link in the food chain. Other larger microorganisms feed on this dish. These, then, attract small invertebrates, which in turn attract small fishes from surrounding waters, which in their turn draw in larger predatory fishes, including the caribes. Snakes, frogs, caimans come too, converting the waters under the nesting trees and bushes into a packed feeding gradient of hungry creatures. It is local legend that no less than five men met a caribe fate in this same garcero during the plume-collecting days. Three had been shot in altercations; two had accidentally fallen out of their canoes. All—and there is no substantial reason to doubt this—had summarily been converted into skeletons by the caribes. I marveled at the nonchalance with which my fellow canoeists faced the ever-present possibility of a similar fate.

That a fish creature seemed in its savage performance to manifest the predominating spirit of the garcero had, perhaps, an element of appropriateness. From the viewpoint of evolutionary seniority, the caribe far outranked both the birds in the trees and us mammals in the dugout. Fishes do in fact constitute the most ancient of vertebrate types, their fossil records extending back some 450,000,000 years. Today they are the dominant fauna of the planet's waters and show greater diversity of form and habit than perhaps any other class of backboned animals. Fishes abound in the depths of the sea, in mid-ocean, at the surface, in the pounding surf. They thrive in quiet lakes, in fast mountain streams, in swamps; and they inhabit the underground waters of caves. Some fishes spend a portion of their lives in salt water, the remainder in fresh. Some have selected the bottom as their habitat, lying on or buried in mud or sand. Some eat nutrient-containing sediment; many are carnivores; others are herbivores. Some species can glide through the air; others can crawl into foliage or onto rocks out of water. Some prefer the warm waters of the tropics, while others choose the near-freezing temperatures of the polar seas or of the abyss. There is hardly an aquatic habitat situation conceivable into which one or more species of fish have not radiated. The pigmentation and iridescence of fishes are not surpassed even by the insects or birds;

and for bizarreness of shape, fish run the morphological gamut.

The earliest known fossil fishes (ostracoderms) had, as their name signifies, a hide of hard shell. Their mouths were but simple holes utterly lacking in jaw structures. The possession of armor plate by an otherwise relatively innocuous form is explained by some paleontologists in the concomitant presence of great scorpionlike predators with powerful biting weapons. Against these, external plate appears to have been the best defense.

Some of these earliest fishes eventually developed jaws. Now equipped with offensive as well as with defensive weapons, they could venture forth from their previous habitat of muddy swamp bottoms for an open life of competitive foraging. Later, probably in the interest of speed and maneuverability, such species lost most of their armor, migrated to the sea, which in those days was a delicatessen of invertebrates, and there became the forebears of present-day sharks.

In a second line of descent, a radical engineering development was introduced. Previously the internal skeleton of fishes consisted of "bones" of pliable, relatively soft, cartilaginous material. The new development involved the replacement of such cartilage with calcium and phosphorous compounds to produce hard bone. This principle of calcification was adopted, wholly or in part, by all animals above fishes in the vertebrate series.

Because of their common ancestry, present-day fishes, amphibians, reptiles, birds and mammals share a number of other features: a dorsally placed hollow nerve trunk, a backbone to house the nerve trunk as well as to support the internal skeleton, and many features of less conspicuous nature. Had I been able to dissect one of those garcero caribes, I should have found an anatomical and physiological equivalent of nearly every structure and system in my own body. That there were no psychological similarities between me and the caribe, I quietly thanked God and an evolutionary process of several hundred million years. Then I thought of the savagery that sometimes breaks forth from the depths of human nature.

Chico's demonstration constituted my first close-up experience with caribes. He saw that I was impressed and a little scared, and that seemed to please him. I must admit, however, that contributing also to my failure immediately to get back into a bird-searching frame of mind was the sight not far off of a pair of eyes peering out from under the swamp's surface scum. A snout barely visible was separated from the eyes by an ominous distance. That distance had somewhat the same significance as the amount of an iceberg extending above the sea; both give reliable clues as to the magnitude of what lies below. Chico straightway identified these visible parts as belonging to a caiman; but for me to have been positively sure that the creature was a member of the caiman rather than of the closely related crocodile genus I would either have had to make the taxonomic test of determining how the fourth tooth on either side of the lower jaw fitted into the upper jaw, or have observed the creature during its nesting period. For caimans (genus *Caiman*), in addition to differing from true crocodiles (genus *Crocodilus*) in a few relatively minor anatomical details, have distinctive nesting habits.

Whereas the crocodile usually lays its eggs in the sun-heated sand of riverbanks, the caiman gathers a mass of leaves and small branches which it proceeds to pile into a nest heap several feet across. The female does all this alone, for after courtship and copulation she and the male have no further association. Before depositing her eggs the female deserts the heap for several days, during which time the fresh foliage, like moist hay, gets warm due to heat released by organic decomposition. Then the builder returns to pull the top layers off the heap and to lay approximately thirty eggs there in a soft, moist, warm nest. She replaces the cover, and from then on the eggs are on their own. After about 70 days in this natural incubator the eggs hatch and the wriggling young, by means of an obscure orientation mechanism, make for the nearest water. In South America there are two species of crocodiles, five of caiman.

During the dry season some of the llanos crocodiles and caimans seek permanent deep-water lagoons; others move from one drying pond to another, gorging themselves on the fish that have become concentrated and are easily captured during this time. Finally, fat and satisfied, the great reptiles bury themselves in the drying mud to rest out the rainless season in a state of semitorpor known as estivation.

The incongruity of birds having descended from reptile-like ancestors was vastly impressive as I observed that member of the Order Crocodilia motionless in the midst of an otherwise predominantly bird world. That birds and reptiles are in fact closely related is indicated by a number of anatomical similarities. Both the Aves and the Crocodilia possess a true four-chambered heart; the gizzard of Crocodilia has the same type of outward-radiating muscle fibers as are found in the bird gizzard; the reptile's scales are anatomically homologous to feathers; both lay shelled or membraned eggs; etc. These facts I had long known, but they became miraculous and almost unbelievable as I noted the difference in design and behavior between that lethargic, heavily armored aquatic monster and those highly metabolic, exquisitely plumed conquerors of the air above me.

Take the matter of that four-chambered heart, a type of pumping plant alone possessed by the crocodiles, birds and mammals. In fishes, at the bottom of the vertebrate series, the heart consists of little more, in principle, than a muscular thickening of the central blood channel, which, by contracting and relaxing in synchrony with the action of appropriately placed one-way valves, forces the blood fluid forward, employing the same principle as the simplest sort of man-made pump. The channel leading from the fish heart goes directly to the gills, where it breaks into branches, then into thin-walled capillaries. Blood passing through these water-bathed gill capillaries releases carbon dioxide along with other wastes, and simultaneously absorbs oxygen. The now-enriched blood is piped on to the body's tissues, from where, having served its physiological purpose, it is returned to the pumping station for a repetition of the cycle.

When animals developed lungs, left the water and embarked on a quasi-terrestrial existence, so simple a heart and so simple a circulatory system were no longer adequate. Amphibians, occupying the rung above fishes on the evolutionary ladder, have what anatomists call a three-chambered heart—two auricles for receiving blood and one heavily musculatured ventricle for pumping it forward. The left auricle receives oxygenated blood from the lungs; the right auricle receives oxygen-depleted blood returning from the muscles, viscera and other body tissues. Both of these blood streams pour into the single ventricle where they cannot avoid undergoing a considerable amount of mixing before being sent back to the lungs, while part of the impure blood, faultily, is returned to the body tissues. Some zoologists think that it was the failure on the part of amphibians to improve on this bad state of ventricular affairs that has forever kept frogs, toads, salamanders, etc., as a backward, nonflourishing type.

The spectacular rise of reptiles to a position of dominance during the Mesozoic certainly had other anatomical, physiological and ecological bases; but it may well have hinged on a simple improvement on the crude pumping system which they inherited from their amphibian forebears. Reptiles developed a curtain, or septum, of tissue down through the center of the ventricle. In this revolutionary conversion of one chamber into two, the whole course of evolution may have been influenced. But while thus improving on the amphibian situation, most reptile groups failed to do a complete job, for the septum was at first imperfect—had a hole in it—and still allowed some admixture of pure and impure blood. Only in the Crocodilia did this hole become sealed over so as to make two perfect blood-tight ventricle chambers.

Not only were the reptile there under the garcero's scum and those birds overhead of one heart, but they were in my league as well, for mammals too have a four-chambered heart. Whether birds and mammals became warm-blooded and metabolically active as a consequence of this, or whether it was the other way around, is not known. But they certainly could not have developed their present physiological efficiency and, in the case of mammals, perhaps their mental alertness if their hearts had remained as hydraulically faulty as those of the amphibians and noncrocodilian reptiles. In the functioning of a complete four-chambered heart, all impure blood returning from the body tissues is immediately pumped to the lungs for oxygenation; then it is hastily returned to the heart for repumping to the oxygen-needing tissues of the body. That simple septum, which created two ventricles where formerly there was but one, may well have been crucial to the speeded-up life patterns of birds and mammals. Why the Crocodilia did not follow up on their monumental endowment is not known. Perhaps it was wisdom.

We had crossed the lagoon, and the canoe pierced the underbrush again. Perhaps the snapping into my face of a leafy branch covered with bird feces helped reorientate me to the world at hand. At any rate, my mind got back to the more pressing matter of locating coro-coros. It comforted me, too, to know that in the heavy foliage here I could at least climb out of reach of caribes and caimans in case of a spill.

We came out into another blue lagoon, and I looked at Chico, pleading that I needed no further caribe entertainment. He was well aware of my primary interest and directed the polesmen to steer a course northward across the lagoon into a low-hung thicket forest under the high trees in which the anhingas nested. Soon we were moving into an area reminiscent of the deep Everglades—shadowed, silent and oppressive. Above us now, but clearing our heads, was a canopy of dense creeper growth. I could see

the trunks of the big anhinga trees, like pilings in the basement of a skyscraper, rising out of the water and penetrating
this secondary foliage in order to reach the open air above.

Here in the shadows were nests of a new variety. They
belonged to boat-billed night herons, a species of marsh
bird forbiddingly homely in repose but suddenly rising to
heights of grace and beauty when in flight. Night herons
were here in enormous abundance, nesting and perching
everywhere. Their bodies were dull blue-black with white
under parts; their beaks, wide and blunt, were like inverted
rowboats; from their heads furled several long feather
streamers which tumbled prettily down over the back and
wings when the birds alighted. Their general behavior was
as quiet and as low-keyed as their habitat; their voices, a
soft *wock-wock*, used sparingly, seemed to intrude as on the
hush of cemetery. Big limpid eyes, like owl eyes for night
foraging, studied us. There must have been at least five
hundred occupied nests piled close in this part of the garcero; and, as we slowly poled through it, a corresponding
number of those great smoky blue orbs were intent on us.

Chico looked up and all around into the branches of
this leafy cavern, then addressed me in Spanish. I did not
get all the words, but I got the sense: "This is where the
coro-coros used to make their nests. But, it seems, no more."
An odd habitat for ibis, I thought; white ibises, at least,
usually prefer the open. Chico directed our pilot to spear
into the tangle again; more machete hacking, disturbed
birds, grunts and pushings as the canoe was forced into,
through and between. Hats were brushed off, clothes seized
by thorns, arms dirtied by rain-soaked accumulations of
excrement. But we went on.

Chico was painfully perplexed. Finally after we had

tunneled what seemed a quarter of a mile and passed into another lagoon, I tried to inquire as to where the white ibises might be nesting. I knew they inhabited the garcero somewhere, for I had seen some thousands flying overhead in reaction to Juan's gunshot. I put my question: *"Donde estan los nidos de los coro-coros blancos?"* Chico passed the inquiry on to the polesman in the stern, who by this time had impressed me as being thoroughly familiar with the details and layout of this garcero maze. The polesman pointed rather vaguely ahead and kept going.

Now in the open again, the magnitude of the garcero was revealed even more fully than before. I had guessed that Juan's shot had flushed about 25,000 birds. This seemed now like too conservative a figure. Literally every bush, tree and thicket endlessly all around was draped with a tapestry of birds, the majority group being, of course, snowy and American egrets.

Now and then I would see two egrets engaging in one aspect or another of their quaint nest-relief ceremony; and with this sight came an understanding of why egret plumes were so dearly sought in the days when ladies' hats needed beautifying. I would see a brooder quietly at rest on her eggs—just a white bird, no more or less handsome than, say, a reposing sea gull. She would suddenly rise to her feet and magically turn into a spray of gleaming tendrils. Back feathers, with shafts standing nearly erect, would become pure snowy gossamer; wings partly ajar would flutter and tremble; head feathers would lift into a regal crest, while those of the lower neck and chest would flow into a trailing beard. At the same time the bird would emit a cry full of plaintive emotion. She would have spotted her mate approaching.

The mate would come into view, racing in across the bush top with wings low, seeming to run on all fours. At the edge of the nest it would stop and become the mirror image of its welcoming mate. Both birds would stand face to face in full display—magnified snowflakes of quite breath-taking beauty. One not familiar with egrets might have construed this behavior as that of two cocks about to do battle. Actually, it was quite the opposite. The two birds were but exhibiting connubial recognition, and perhaps even a variety of affection. There was some posturing, some crossing of bills and necks; then the brooder, still standing directly over the eggs, would gently step aside so that its mate could take over. The newcomer would eagerly probe and turn the eggs, then relax its plumes and lower its body. Its mate would soon fly off for its turn at feeding in distant shallows. I could not tell, actually, which sex was which, for male and female egrets look identical.

Courtship is something which for most animal species, and indeed often in human society, is regarded as a pre-mating device aimed either at winning favor or at inducing sexual stimulation—an intimate rapport to be engaged in as a preamble to copulation. Yet, among many a monogamous bird species, display is practiced long after the initial mating and, as in the case of egrets, may persist until the young are fledged. This nest-relief ceremony of egrets, although clearly an extension or derivation of courting behavior, has apparently attained some meaning beyond that of mere sexual stimulation.

"Marriage" among birds, as among mammals, is extremely complex and varied. Parrots and ravens are said to practice lifelong monogamy; many birds are monogamous for only one season at a time. There is evidence that most sea birds have the same mate over a period of years. Some birds, pheasants for example, are polygamous, each male winning and dominating a harem; while yet other species are wholly promiscuous. Among the polygamists, males are often gaudily attired and capable of extravagant displays, whereas the females are drab, giving rise to a high degree of competitiveness among the males. In such seasonally monogamous birds as egrets, display cannot be considered a device for competitive sexual selection, for both sexes are equally plumed and engage in mutual display. Birds of solitary nesting habit often pursue their courtship activities clandestinely some distance from the nest site, presumably so as not to reveal its location to watching nest robbers. Among gregarious birds, where the rookery's location is known to all, courtship and display may take place near the nest in full view of all observers. Incidentally, plumage display is only one of a number of stimulating devices of value in bird courtship. Some species engage in elaborate dances, others in the presentation of sticks, stones or even food. In yet other species one member of the courting pair may find stimulation in running off and being chased, or in song, or in all manner of peckings and cooings.

Whereas such prenuptial activity in birds is supposedly set off, or "released," by the action of endocrine glands, notably the anterior pituitary and the gonads, there are no doubt many other influences at play too. Diet, climate, length of day and night, temperature, hormonal rhythms, etc., have been studied in considerable detail, but their specific bearings on the physiology and psychology of bird reproduction are still subject to investigation and debate. Why, for example, do some birds—specifically the various species I was observing—gather in such overwhelming numbers and in such dense concentration? Water birds of the egret, heron, ibis and anhinga groups exhibit no extreme gregariousness during the interbreeding period. A number of individuals may roost in common trees or feed in loose flock formations, but during the summertime they are generally to be found scattered over the face of the llanos and indeed the whole Orinoco basin. What, when the floods come, impels them to assemble and nest in great cities?

The question is an old and nettling one in the field of animal behavior. The effect of hormones on migration, nuptial behavior, nesting, egg laying, brooding, postnatal care of young, etc., would appear to a considerable extent to be superimposed on the more deeply imprinted genetic behavior pattern of each species. And it is this superimposition that makes the problem so complex. In one case, hormone releasers will impel a bird species to migrate, in another to stay where it is; in one, to build a solitary nest, in another to join the crowd; in one, to select a single partner, or in yet another to round up a harem.

Here in this garcero there was no sign of organized social behavior such as is found, for example, among the ants and termites. No individuals were serving the group need. There was no queen or leader. Nor could one conclude that the proximity of a common food supply was the impelling magnet, for miles of unrestricted feeding shallows all around lay dotted with a myriad other trees and foliage islands that some of the birds could have chosen as nesting sites. Nor was it a common pooling of resources against any sort of natural foe that drew the birds together. Not one of these cared a whit whether the inhabitant of a neighboring nest lived or died. The sociology of birds is nearly as complex as that of men, and about as murkily understood.

We were approaching the lagoon's far end where another wall of thicket loomed up. The soldiers were becoming a little restless; it was almost noon, and siesta time was near. Chico's bottle (he had, fortunately, brought only one) had long since died a natural death. But we had not yet come to the ibis section of the garcero; until then, I would not give up. My wait was a short one, for some white specks, which from a distance I had construed as egrets, turned out to be ibises—not the scarlet variety, to be sure, but the closest approximation yet. When we were near enough to flush them, Chico called out loudly; and hungry and sleepy Juan, to speed things up, fired his revolver into the air again. Immediately there was a repetition of the effect wrought by the earlier shot. The ibises had risen en masse, at least several thousand of them, creating a brilliant whiteness broken only by the flickering of black-tipped wing feathers. These birds flew in closer and more exclusive formation than the egrets and herons. Their wings beat faster, and, with long, curved-down beaks thrust forward, they spiraled high and round and round. I studied the sky, alert for signs of scarlet in those whorls.

Eventually when the birds had settled, Chico turned to me, shrugged his shoulders and, with admirable honesty, summarized the situation with "No coro-coros." Abruptly he instructed the polesmen to reverse course and head back to the river. If I had not already had nine similarly negative experiences to my credit, I suppose I should have felt some bitterness. As it was, I went along with the attitude implicit in Chico's shoulder shrug. With consistency, the results of this day's search were falling into line behind the earlier ones. By this time I had indeed come to doubt the books, Phelps, Urbano, Delgado, Chico—any and all sources of scarlet-ibis lore.

A well-known explorer has made the statement that adventure during the course of an exploration is a sign of amateurishness or lack of preparation. A properly thought-out and discreetly conducted expedition, he says, should function like clockwork, without melodrama, danger or failure. My own feeling is that if the outcome of an expedition is finely predictable, we are not dealing with exploration. True exploration—whether in a geographic or a laboratory setting—must by its very essence have elements of high unpredictability.

I say—and here I am on the defensive—that my repeated failure to locate the scarlet ibis was due not to inadequate or faulty planning, nor to bad field management. The breeding habits and habitats of most animals are well recorded, and one need only consult the literature for details as to time, place and special conditions. But when one tries, even with background material of the sort supplied by the Phelpses, to locate the nesting grounds of an exotic bird species whose habits are moot, he is likely to encounter hazards and uncertainties that he had no way of anticipating. If, in short, he wishes to blaze a trail, he is likely—I may say certain—to encounter disappointment, hazard and failure—sometimes, with God's special help, success. So far God had not seen fit to favor me.

This was the sort of rationalizing I resorted to at the end of my second day of searching in Chico's garcero. Alone and unintimidated by doubt, caribe or caiman, the two peon polesmen and I had returned to the garcero. If we missed examining a single tree or bush, I should be surprised. There just were no red birds, although without doubt they had been there in previous years. This particular year happened to be an aberrant one. Obviously some "x" factor during the current season was responsible for the absence of the scarlet ibis from its usual haunts along the Río Apure.

For a time I thought of giving up and going home. Was a little red bird ample justification for exposing myself further to caribes, crocodiles, caimans, disease, filth, parasites, pests, rain, flood and a military escort? That evening at Chico's I lay in my hammock, not quite but almost convinced that my search must end. Then I heard shouts of *"Amigo!"* outside on the riverbank.

I got up and saw my Arichuna friend's canoe turning into shore. My state of mind somehow had foolishly led me to expect a miracle: perhaps Blecker would announce that he himself had found the red birds, that I need seek no further. Instead, he greeted me and said that he had made the trip downriver to pay me a visit and to help me with the coro-coros, which by now I must surely have located. I related the events of the past two days. Blecker quizzed Chico for a time and at last said to me, "Well, you need stay here no longer. Come, let us put your things into my boat and return to Arichuna. Rest up there with me. We will visit the two or three small garceros around Arichuna. If we do not find any red birds there, I will take you back to San Fernando for a talk with my friend Don Carlos."

More running around in circles, more fruitless consultations would have been the normal reaction to this, in my

state of mind. But somehow having someone I could talk
to again had a rejuvenating effect on my spirit. Yes, perhaps we would still find the birds. I forgot the radiogram
that I had already composed in my mind for sending to the
National Geographic Society from San Fernando, and
decided gratefully to go along with Dr. Blecker.

To my surprise, Juan and his companion did not restrain
me, nor did they insist on coming along. I was told they
had another mission to perform downriver and would
surely look me up in Arichuna when they finished that job.

"My wife in Germany often writes that I should send
for her," Dr. Blecker was saying as we dined that evening
in the native Arichuna hut where he took his meals. The
floor, as usual, was solid-packed dirt, although this hut,
the home of a dark-faced, barefooted matron who cooked
for the doctor, seemed a little tidier than most others I had
been in. Of course there were chickens on the floor and a
wormy dog or two; and occasionally a beetle, dropping
from out of the peaked thatch ceiling, would thump down
onto the oilclothed table. And that religious calendar on
the wall. I had seen similar ones at Chico's and in other
llanos huts. The designers and distributors of such calen-
dars have a keen adaptive sense, for the complexions of
the saints pictured were as dark as any llanero's. I remember a calendar in my home when I was a boy; the complexions of the saints on that one were a glowing Caucasian
white.

"But who would bring a European woman here to Arichuna?" Blecker continued, sweeping his arms broadly so
as to include the unsalted soup we were eating, the creatures on the floor, the hut, the village, the river, the

flooded lands outside. He went on to explain that he had married during the war but had not seen his wife for so long that he hardly remembered what she looked like. Perhaps someday he would be in a position to send for her. The government paid him an extra-high salary in return for his being stationed at so primitive an outpost. Living cost him nothing here; he could bank almost his entire income in San Fernando. By next year, furthermore, his ranch should yield perhaps fifty cattle, each with a market value of close to a hundred dollars; before long, if the project thrived, he should be able to clear $15,000 per annum from cattle alone. Considering the negligibility of an income tax in Venezuela, he would be a wealthy man in ten years and could settle down in Caracas or go to America.

"But do you think your wife will wait that long?"

He smiled and said jokingly, "If she does not, I can always marry some nice Venezuelan girl from Caracas." Then, changing the subject, he said, "Tomorrow afternoon we go to my ranch. There I will send my peons to examine the garceros. If red birds are discovered, Arichuna will become your headquarters."

Next morning I went to Dr. Blecker's office with him. The low structure, once white, was crudely roofed with tile and surrounded by mud and puddles. A small gathering of barefoot folk was already waiting out in front, as at any public clinic anywhere, mostly mothers with babes in arms. Blecker's nurse, the neatest woman I had seen since my arrival in the llanos, was busy opening the doors and windows, getting ready for the morning's business. I was surprised at the amount of medical equipment within: glass-fronted cabinets containing instruments for minor surgery, sterilizing baths, a standard examination table, etc. Dr. Blecker had told me he did not do major surgery here; serious cases were canoed upriver to the central hospital at San Fernando.

Sepsis and contamination were the doctor's dilemma. The walls inside the treatment room were peeling from damp-rot; the enamel white of the new instrument cases already had patches of rust. The cement floor was sweating moisture. One felt that spores of bacteria and fungi were floating free and unrestrained everywhere. "Now it is fungus rot that gets into everything," Blecker was saying. "In the dry season it is dust." Even minor surgery is risky, he went on, but made less so these days only by the availability of antibiotics. It occurred to me how impotent the modern medical man—llanos or Park Avenue—would be without someone to provide him with those wonderfully standardized and sterile packages of medicinals ready for immediate ingestion or injection.

I left the *médico* to his patients and went wandering about the village. He would be through by noon, and then we would go to the ranch. As I idled, I saw vultures by the dozens circling overhead or perched ominously on nearly every hut top; I saw potbellied children who should have been over in the clinic being dewormed; I saw pools of stagnant water, pigs lolling in filthy mud; I saw citizens whose eyes were slow and sleepy from an internal fauna and flora of parasitic things. I thought of those up-to-date ampules fresh out of civilization's pharmaceutical laboratories available to these people but for the asking only a minute's walk away, and again I thought of the inscription above the door of that San Fernando schoolhouse.

That afternoon we rode horseback to the ranch several

miles inland from Arichuna. It consisted of a rather vast
stretch of half-flooded savanna, sprinkled here and there
with patches of jungle forest and green and blue lagoons.
This, like most of the Apure-basin llanos, was bird-feeding
country; the horizon was speckled with dots of white and
gray-blue. There were a few cows not far off wading up to
their bellies, munching on grass tops. Here on the flooded
flats, caribes apparently did not penetrate. The ranch house
was not unlike other llanos dwellings I had seen and lived
in, although one section had a new tin roof and inside a
new cement floor. This was no concession to human comfort, Blecker explained, but rather a place in which to store
grain and corn against thieving rodents.

We were scarcely off our horses when a great to-do broke
out from somewhere behind the house. There we found
that one of the peons had cornered a two-foot-long iguana
lizard in a chicken enclosure and was now in the process
of beating it to death with a stick. "That man is saving
fifty eggs for me," Blecker remarked casually, as though
this sort of thing were an everyday occurrence. At the
house, coffee was brought by a girl whose rather good
looks were damaged by sizable feet and an unwashed neck.
She was housekeeper and cook. When we arrived I had
noticed her, untidily clad, yelling savagely at the lizard
beater to beat harder. Now, bringing us our coffee, she was
in a clean dress and her lips were reddened with something
straight out of a llanos Woolworth's.

Peons (nonowners of land, as distinguished from land-
owning llaneros) do all the menial work here in the llanos
country—which, in this instance, after all my swamp crawling and cramped river travel, pleased me very much. Furthermore, I had found that for a nonpeon to do physical

work is not appreciated as a sign of democratic philosophy; rather, one loses the peon's respect and even becomes subject to his ridicule. In this back country there is still a strong residuum of feudal psychology in practice. I remembered how Chico a number of times had looked at me askance and uncomprehending as I started to hang my own hammock or to lift some parcel for myself. Always he would call a peon to relieve me of the need for any such degrading exertion. On the other hand, there are jobs that are respectable for, indeed exclusive to, the higher castes: running or taking care of an outboard, for example, or handling a good gun or a special horse, or drinking sealed liquor. The line between respectability and vulgarity is a fine but absolute one. In the urban centers of Venezuela this system of social stratification is tumbling with almost revolutionary swiftness. But the wave front of reform has not yet effectively hit the deep llanos.

Only signs of cattle activity at the Blecker ranch were an empty corral and a few saddles perched up under the eaves of the house. When at the end of winter the water retreated and the llanos became dry, then the world here would awaken and the Venezuelan equivalent of our western roundup would begin. Each llanero and his peons would mount their small swift horses and drive in the cattle, segregate them, select those ready for market, castrate most of the male calves and escort the year's crop to staging areas from which the dwindling Apure would be forded. Then in great composite herds the cattle would be driven on the long journey across dusty prairie country to abattoirs in the north.

There were three peons in residence at Blecker's place. With blank, perhaps quizzical, faces they listened to their master's orders that they visit every garcero and bird tree within horse and canoe range and to report on the presence of coro-coros. I had brought my hammock along from Arichuna, half expecting to stay at the ranch while the bird hunt was on. But now I could see no reason for doing so. Furthermore, Blecker persuaded, his peons would bring their report directly to him at Arichuna. I think he wanted my company; I know I wanted his. So by early evening we were both back in Arichuna.

The peons followed two days later, driving three pigs before them and also carrying word that not a coro-coro was to be found in the whole district this season. I was not particularly surprised by this information, by now having become quite resigned to the fact that my search would have to shift drastically elsewhere. I had already more or less made up my mind to follow one or all of three plans: the first, to return to San Fernando and call on the Governor of Apure for official aid; the second, to fly to Caracas for a conference with Señor Ramella, who, at the Phelps party, had said that in case of trouble he would contribute the use of his airplane to my search; the third, suggested by Blecker, to go see his influential friend Don Carlos in San Fernando.

Accordingly, on the fourth day after leaving Chico's place, Dr. Blecker and I found ourselves, together with all my luggage, in the doctor's canoe for the dawn-to-dusk trip upriver to the capital city. With us were the three pigs from Blecker's farm on their way to market in San Fernando. With legs thoroughly trussed, they lay in the dugout's wet bottom, grunting, defecating and generally competing with our feet and my luggage for space.

The excursion was concluded without incident and that

night I was installed again at the Hotel Grande. This time the realisms of the place went unnoticed. Indeed, I had picked up enough Spanish since my earlier visit to permit elementary banter with the managing *señora* and her buxom aide.

I had hardly accepted the welcoming cup of coffee when a uniformed visitor arrived to announce that I was to report at headquarters before noon the next day.

Next morning at ten o'clock, instead of going to the police, I went directly to the quarters of the Governor of the state of Apure. I had two rather pressing matters on my mind: to try to get out from under all this mysterious military attention, and to lay my scarlet-ibis dilemma before official eyes. The seersucker suit I wore for the occasion was clean but disgracefully wrinkled. Nevertheless, for the llanos, I was so dandily overdressed that various street ladies gave the Spanish equivalent of a low wolf whistle as I walked past. I knew that every eye was on my daring and unprecedented use of a necktie.

The Governor's "mansion" was not much different from any other middle-class dwelling in San Fernando. It lay behind one of those peeling white walls which rise like low palisades out of every San Fernando sidewalk to form an eaved continuum from one end of each block to the other. I knew I had come to the right place when I saw two military guards, with the familiar rifles and side arms, lounging on chairs before a closed door. Despite my not having an appointment, I was admitted without fuss or card and escorted to an inside garden surrounded by the usual open-sided, cement-floored verandas.

People were lined up under the eaves along one side of

The caribe of Venezuela, the piranha of Brazil, the perai of British Guiana, all belong to a genus of small freshwater fish reputed to be the most ferocious of its size in the world. When the naturalist Humboldt described the caribe as "one of the greatest scourges of these climes," he was specifically referring to the Apure River basin where my Scarlet Ibis were awaiting me.

Among the distant trees nested thousands of waterbirds—but, alas, no coro-coros.

The crocodile family once may have been more abundant in the llanos, but the traveller must still keep his eyes open when near tall grass close to the river.

The high half-skeletonized trees were full of occupied anhinga nests.

My llanos friends pose pleasantly for a snapshot.

This llanos lizard will visit the hen coop no more.

Cattle could be seen in deep along the banks of the swollen river, munching on grass tips.

With us in the canoe went hoofed pork for the market.

The doctor's nurse, the neatest woman I had seen since my arrival in the llanos, had just opened the doors and windows, and the clinic was ready for business.

the garden, mostly women and children—political petition-
ers awaiting an audience with the Governor, I supposed.
They looked peculiarly like those I had seen at Blecker's
Arichuna clinic a few days before. I had thought that the
Governor's title of "Dr." referred to the practice of law, for
in Venezuela most licensed lawyers, or *abogados,* have university degrees in jurisprudence and commonly use the doc-
torate title.

That a medical and not a legal variety of doctor was in
charge of the state of Apure was evident a few minutes
later when a comparatively young man with an alert face
stepped out of the doorway where the women and children
were lined up. He was dressed in the white clothes of a
surgeon. His collar was open and, like the rest of us, he was
perspiring profusely from the heat. Dr. E. F. Dominguez
combined a career of politics and medicine, and did so very
competently, I was told later. The soldier, obviously having
informed the Governor of my presence, pointed me out and
then retired. The man in white came over.

In view of the language barrier and the absence of a
translator, I just handed him my papers—those by now
somewhat dog-eared letters of introduction and authentica-
tion. He gave me a piercing look, then sat down at the little
round drugstore table near by to read. Once or twice he
directed some Spanish at me; then, seeing that I did not
comprehend, he smiled and continued to read. At length
he handed the papers back, excused himself and disappeared through a doorway leading into what I gathered
were his living quarters, for I caught glimpses of strung
hammocks.

Reappearing shortly, Dr. Dominguez was accompanied
by a striking young woman, taller than he, blond, thor-

oughly Nordic. He introduced her as *"Mi Señora."* She immediately took charge, speaking a halting but perfect English. Yes, she was the Governor's wife, of German extraction and educated in England. She said she longed for the day she and her husband and children could return to a more comfortable life in Caracas. The llanos climate did not agree with her, she added, punctuating the statement with a sharp look at a black vulture that had just landed on the garden mud.

The Governor stood by quietly during the exchange of these pleasant but irrelevant amenities, then spoke briefly to her. She turned to me again: "My husband says you are very welcome to the state of Apure. It is hot and miserable here now, but in summer it is dry and even pleasant. He says you must visit us then sometime. We have a fine Ambassador in Washington, and a fine Consul General in New York. My husband wonders how you will find such birds as you seek unless you can speak the language of the peons."

I related the history of my searches so far, emphasizing the courteous and helpful treatment I had been accorded by peon and llanero alike, even without being able to converse with them. She translated this information back to the Governor. A servant had appeared with a tray of coffee which he placed on the little table. Señora Dominguez continued that her husband knew nothing of the bird life of Apure, although he believed many interesting varieties were to be found here. However, he would inquire. Meanwhile, I should feel that San Fernando was my home. He would let me know in a day or two, after he had made inquiries as to where best to look for the scarlet birds.

Throughout the conversation I could not help being

aware of a sense of amazement and incredulity on the part of the Governor that anyone should have come all the way from the United States to this flooded hot Apure land, impelled by nothing more important than birds. While I conversed with the *señora*, the Governor took the papers from my hand and again carefully read the letter from the Venezuela Ambassador to confirm, no doubt, that my mission here was authentic.

The coffee was finished, and the conversation ended abruptly. In a minute I was outside walking down the street. Then I remembered that I had completely forgotten to mention the military complications in my life, that I was in trouble again.

When I returned to my hotel preparatory to yielding to the military summons, I was surprised to find the message bearer of the previous evening waiting there, all smiles and humility. He said that everything was now in order; no need for me to report. It was as obvious as the overhearing ear of the Hotel Grande's proprietress that a wondrously efficient grapevine operated between the Governor's house and the headquarters of the *Guardia Nacional.*

Chapter 4

THE CENTRAL SQUARE, or plaza, of San Fernando is the city's pulsing heart, indeed in some respects that of the entire state of Apure. All visitors and a goodly proportion of the local citizenry gather there during the late afternoon of every day. When there is no rain, the square functions as a fresh-air cocktail lounge; when there is, the customer merely hugs close under the big umbrella that sprouts up through the middle of each table until the shower is over. In the center of the square, as in any proper country town, is a bandstand with cement walks spoking out from it. Bordering the whole is a narrow pavement for vehicles.

The square is situated a few feet above the ordinary high-water mark of the river and is shaded and cooled somewhat by a number of well-foliaged trees. Along with a government building to the south and an ancient business edifice to the north near the wharf, a number of small shops, eating places and cervecerías surround this central plexus of San Fernando. The cervecerías turn it each evening into a social magnet. Each cervecería has its own area of iron tables, remotely administered by a waiter staff of barefoot urchin runners.

I have said that the kerosene refrigerator is having a revolutionary effect on life in the llanos. Equally tradition-breaking is the postwar American jeep, which is rapidly coming to comprise a dominant fauna here. The jeep, with its powered four-wheel drive, is about the only conveyance other than the oxcart or donkey cart that can long endure the rigors of winter mud or the wear of summer chuckholes. That the genus *Jeep* had taken over in San Fernando was particularly evident to me as I sat on this evening at one of the cervecería tables, for there was a continuous parade of these inelegant, mud-spattered quadrupeds slowly stalking around the square. Some were loaded with gay young men in search of feminine company, others with *el señor, la señora* and *los* many *niños.* During the floods this is about the only place a San Fernandan can go for an evening's drive with the family; out of town the pavement ribbons are soon replaced by mud and water.

It was neither relaxation nor the need for refreshment that accounted for my presence here on this occasion. Nor was I observing jeep life with anything more than a casual interest. I sat with my eyes and ears unavoidably open, but with my thoughts on a radiotelephone conversation I had had a while before with Billy Phelps in Caracas.

I had explained my failure to find the scarlet ibises where Urbano had seen them the year before and how subsequently and unsuccessfully I had scoured the Apure countryside. Since there were no small planes for charter here in San Fernando, did he (Billy) think that Señor Ramella could be persuaded to bring or send his plane for an aerial search?

Billy was a little taken aback by the first item of information, saying he thought that by this time I would be almost through with my job. As to the second, Billy said that he would get in touch with Ramella and call me back next day.

I had left the radio station and, while passing across the

square, decided to sit down and ponder my frustrations and
problems. It was about this time that one of those jeeps
stopped not far from where I sat. Out stepped my friend
Blecker. He said he had been looking for me all afternoon.
Don Carlos had heard of me and my ibis troubles and
would be happy to be informed of them firsthand this very
evening. Was I free now? I said yes, got up and hopped into
the jeep, and we were off. Numbers one and two of my
three plans had been set into motion; the third was at that
moment being initiated.

Don Carlos Rodriguez Rincones had been in previous
years Governor of the state of Apure, but his political fortunes had faded with the coming of the present administra-
tion. He owned a ranch of considerable size downriver and
was regarded as one of San Fernando's more substantial
citizens. It was Don Carlos' mentorship, apparently, that
had got Blecker started in cattle. However, Don Carlos, like
the Río Apure, had had ups and downs. A few years earlier
he had been nearly wiped out during one of the seasonal
floods when some 5,000 head of his cattle, worth a half-
million dollars, were lost.

The Don Carlos characterization by Blecker had somewhat led me to expect palaces and estates. Actually, his
San Fernando house, only two blocks east of the square,
was typical; there were no servants, no external signs of
affluence. Don Carlos' wife lived in Caracas, and his daughter attended school in the United States. He himself preferred the earthy informality of the llanos.

When we arrived, the former Governor was lounging
deep in a veranda hammock reading a book. The far side of
the courtyard, I could see, had been converted into a sort

of garage for outboard motors; there were tool benches, fuel tanks, other appurtenances of a shop, and a rack of motors. What, in addition, distinguished these quarters radically was the presence along one wall of the court of two stalls, one equipped with a shower and the other with a conventional toilet. This was an advancement for these parts and gave a clue to the owner's sense of refinement. Parenthetically, the conspicuous lack of good plumbing in this part of the world is due in large measure to too much water in winter, too little in summer. The disposal problems introduced by such a situation would frustrate the best of sanitation engineers. How they were solved in this case I never learned.

Don Carlos was a small but well-built man with a stern, scholarly face which in conversation became warm and sympathetic. He received us graciously. He could speak a little English, plainly wanted to learn more, and tried hard to express at least the amenities in my tongue rather than his own. But before long Dr. Blecker had taken over as interpreter; the weather, my new model of outboard, the United States, the daughter's school in Pennsylvania were topics touched on. We were about to get to the reason for my visit to Apure when several other gentleman visitors arrived, one of whom Don Carlos shoulder-patted most warmly and then described to me as his very best friend in all the world.

This man looked like any other respectable llanero—sandaled feet, short white trousers, belt-held knife holster, chin-secured sombrero, etc. He rattled on in fast Spanish like the others, then suddenly turned and began speaking to me in the King's English. He had been introduced earlier, but I had failed to get the name. Now I learned that he was Mr. H. L. E. Briggs, the superintendent of a chain of llanos cattle ranches operated by a British syndicate.

Before long we were on the subject of scarlet ibises, and at this point Don Carlos asked Briggs to translate what I was saying into Spanish. Carlos and his sombreroed guests listened thoughtfully as I spoke through Mr. Briggs. I launched headlong into my story: the auspicious start, the early difficulties in San Fernando, the various sorties up and down river, the running bad luck. At first the listeners nodded gravely at each point Briggs made, then slowly I was aware of the barest twinkle coming into Don Carlos' eyes. Briggs and I talked on: the rarity of the scarlet ibis, its alleged beauty, its nests, number of eggs, the incubation period. . . . The lines around Don Carlos' mouth were stretching into a grin. We continued: the probable diet of the scarlet ibis, its down-curved beak . . .

With this, finally, Don Carlos broke into laughter, in which he was heartily joined by the others. Even Blecker, who had taken all my earlier accounts to him in German with courteous solemnity, was loudly amused. The humor seemed to originate in the improbable concept of a grown man trying to locate a little red bird and going to such extreme lengths of personal discomfort to do so. Charlie Chaplin has said that all true humor must have an element of pathos; I seemed unconsciously to be supplying this. Each word now seemed to gain in pungency as I recounted for Briggs my canoe adventures, the ibis-empty garceros, my despair over not finding that for which I had abandoned family and laboratory and come 3,000 miles. I could not, of course, tell what slants or asides Briggs was inserting into my text, but I do know that the net effect was one of

holding the assembled company in a state of good humor
for nearly an hour—humor which at times reached the
point of producing risible tears in the eyes of these men
who usually wore fiercely solemn faces. No longer of scholarly and ex-gubernatorial mien, Don Carlos seemed to consider this the most beguiling thing he had heard in years.
"More beers for everyone," he said. "No, I will open some
of my oldest cognac."

I did not realize it at the time, but this hour was to be
crucial to my entire bird search. Had I been piqued by the
hilarious response to my story, I should then and there
have spoiled my chance. As it was, two things seemed to
save the day for me: first, by exerting a degree of self-con-
trol ordinarily out of reach for me, I joined in the laughter
at myself, which in llanos psychology is a nice thing to be
able to do; second, I drank the proffered refreshment at
rapid llanero pace and, in complete defiance of the laws
of physiological absorption, showed, so far as I know, no
overt signs of intoxication. The latter feat, I learned later,
pleased Don Carlos.

I have never ceased being impressed by the role played
in the lives of men by a relatively simple molecule consisting of two atoms of carbon, six of hydrogen and one of oxygen. Be it at a cocktail party on Sutton Place, in the living
room of a middle-class home, under the grape arbor of a
Sicilian peasant's hut, along the Bowery or in the llanos of
Venezuela, alcohol gives a stimulus to life that nature forgot to provide. The paradox is that alcohol is, physiologically, a depressant, not a stimulant.

Depressed or stimulated, it was not long before Don
Carlos began breaking into Briggs's translation with some
pointed questions: Where else in the world is this *"eebis*

escarlata" to be found? Had this treasure been all this time
in his native Apure without Don Carlos knowing about it?
Why did the National Geographic Society wish to have pictures of this bird? Was the scarlet ibis related to the sacred
ibis of Egypt?

I answered these questions as fully as I could. Then
slowly I began to feel that I had stood up under fire. Both
Don Carlos and Mr. Briggs seemed sincerely concerned
over my difficulties. Furthermore, I had afforded them an
evening's diversion, which during the wet season of bored
waiting is worth something.

It was then that Briggs disclosed that peons at one of
his company's outlying ranches on the Río Matillure, about
100 miles southwestward from San Fernando, had for years
been telling what he (Briggs) had thought were tall tales
of bushes blood-red with birds out in the middle of a swamp.
Don Carlos, whom I had told of my Caracas connections,
said that if my friend would bring his plane to San Fernando, this matter could be checked within a few hours.
Otherwise, I was in for a long, lonesome river trip. In the
meantime, said Carlos, there were two well-known llaneros
from that same area now in town, the Bezara brothers.
Surely they would be able to shed light on the reliability
of the report. He would send a messenger for them, and
did.

The Bezara brothers soon joined the party. Introduced to
me as the greatest *tigre* hunters in the llanos, these Bezaras
looked the part. They were perfectly enormous, each well
over six feet tall and massive to match, and made to seem
even larger in comparison with the modest size of the
others present. Their father had been a Turkish immigrant,
their mother a Venezuelan. In facial mien they had a fierce-

ness that should have caused any self-respecting tiger to run for cover. That a tiger once hadn't was revealed when, at Briggs's behest, Rafael Bezara stripped the shirt off his back to show me scars of wounds inflicted by the open claws of a great cat's paws. Then the man parted his hair to reveal another scar arced clear across the scalp. "The pate was ripped off down as far as the forehead by the same tiger," Mr. Briggs told me.

I never got the whole story, but it seems that in the course of one of his innumerable hunts Rafael had come too close to what he thought was a fatally shot tiger. The stunned animal regained consciousness just as Rafael was picking her up, and a wrestling match ensued between tiger and man. That the latter had won in the end was indicated by Rafael's current presence. But those scars were impressive evidence that the fight had not been one-sided.

Conversation got back to birds. Yes, both the Bezara brothers were familiar with the coro-coro species. During the summertime there was not a lagoon on their ranch lands without a few red feeders scattered among the white and gray ones. Now in winter they were not often to be seen because, of course, there were no isolated lagoons. One of the Bezaras said he too had heard of the garcero referred to by Briggs and knew several peons who he thought had actually visited it. Language and translation difficulties prevented me from cross-examining these dour-faced men effectively, but this much I did learn: the garcero was about 25 miles up the Río Matillure from Matapalos (the Briggs ranch) and 15 miles from the Bezara ranch settlement. Nor was it located on the bank of the river, but rather in a swamp northwardly inland, where, like most other garceros, it would be accessible only by poled canoe.

Don Carlos looked at me: there you have it, the look said. First, you must confirm the presence of the garcero from the air, then organize a river expedition from San Fernando. To this thought Briggs added in substance: With your 10-hp motor it will take you about three days of river travel to reach Matapalos. I will give you a letter to my manager there, John Kitson. He will help you get in touch with those peons who are supposed to know where the garcero is. But, yes, by all means, check it first from the air if you can.

The air matter was settled for me the next afternoon. About five o'clock a messenger from the radio station came with the information that a call from Caracas awaited me. Señor Ramella had been advised by flight authorities against landing on the San Fernando airfield with his small plane this time of year. Had it been summer, Billy said, Ramella would have been glad to come; now, during the floods, it did not seem wise.*

I left the station and, walking by way of the Governor's house, I ventured in. The Governor received me kindly, as before. He had talked to various people. All were acquainted with the coro-coro (the familiar story) and, had it been summer, could by jeep have driven me to any number of water holes not far outside San Fernando and there have shown me red birds by the dozen. But now, during the floods, *quien sabe?*

That evening when I reported back to Briggs and Don

---

* The following dispatch appeared in the *New York Times* of April 25, 1954: "Dr. Lopez (Dr. Rafael Ernesto Lopez, Venezuelan Consul General in New York at the time of these events) left Caracas, Venezuela, by plane on a hunting trip with Ramella Vegas (Senor Ramella), a wealthy Venezuelan sportsman, and two other men. When the plane became overdue, search craft were sent out and they finally spotted the badly wrecked plane in the jungle."

Subsequent information indicates that the crash, occurring in the llanos presumably due to bad weather, had been fatal to all members of the party.

Carlos the former added an item of encouraging information. Kitson had a plane at Matapalos, a tiny Cessna, which
he ordinarily used only during the summer when fields and
pastures were dry. But Kitson was an adventurous soul,
Briggs said, and might easily be coaxed to take it into the
air for me.

I decided to gamble on the correctness of the Briggs-
Bezara thesis. I would make the trip to Matapalos. Failing
to find my birds there, I would return to Caracas—perhaps
admit defeat and go home.

Two days later at a mudbank east of town I waited for
Briggs and Don Carlos to arrive, for they had insisted on
seeing me off. At length their jeep pulled up, and the two
men came over. I noticed immediately that Don Carlos had
something on his mind. I thought perhaps it was apprehension over the depth to which my boat had sunk under
its load. But no, it never is in the llanos. He reached into a
pocket and drew out two newspaper clippings. While I
read them, Briggs explained that they had been cut from
a recent Caracas paper.

American scientist, I read in essence, unable to find the
scarlet ibis in the state of Apure. After three weeks of
searching and an examination of a dozen different garceros
along the wild Río Apure, the *norteamericano* saw not a
single . . . etc. The other clipping was a reader's Letter
to the Editor asserting that this American had been ill
advised in going to the state of Apure for his red birds in
the first place. Scarlet ibises are to be found along the coast
in the state of Monagas, or perhaps in the state of Guárico.
But never in the state of Apure.

Don Carlos' expression was one of amused displeasure
over this slur on his state. Coro-coros were of course native

to Apure, the only problem being to find the right garcero. Suddenly now the ridiculous matter of a man searching for a bird seemed to take on a nationalist meaning. The prestige of the state of Apure was at stake. Carlos patted my shoulder with vigor, and I felt his thoughts: Good fortune, my friend. Find the coro-coros. Show the doubters. *Viva* Apure!

I started the motor, someone gave the boat a shove, and I was off.

A dozen times during the next three days I prayed inwardly both to heaven and to my outboard. The boat was a little flat-bottom bug—the only such craft in San Fernando—which I had rented as more suited than a heavy dugout to the limited power of my motor. Sitting perched in the prow was a silent peon named Tomás, who knew the way to Matapalos and was serving as my baquiano, or guide. The boat was too heavily loaded and, despite the wide-open throttle, would not rise to a planing angle during the first day. This was wicked on fuel. Not that to run out of gas here would have involved mortal disaster, for we could always float with the current and eventually reach some habitation downriver, where at least we would not starve. But to secure more fuel would have involved literally weeks of waiting while someone paddled a dugout back to San Fernando.

For a full nine hours, from eleven in the morning to nightfall of that first day, we pushed ahead—down the Apure, by pole and paddle through the grass of a great flooded savanna which separates the parallel Apure and Arauca rivers, then heavily against the current up the Arauca. Rather than make camp in the wild that night,

I turned in to a bank clearing where between jungle and river's edge there was an abandoned native hut. Here we hung our hammocks until dawn.

It was in the afternoon of the next day that my thoughts of gratitude toward the motor grew sentimental. By now we had consumed enough of our fuel load so that the bow was beginning to break up over the water, and the boat accordingly took on added speed. The little motor had missed so far not a single cycle, despite hour piled on hour of full-throttle punishment.

Except for the occasional sight or sound of a flying bird, the green drapery on either bank was silent and seemingly uninhabited. This was most striking whenever I would turn off the motor for refueling. Nor was it the mere contrast that made those jungle heaps seem sepulchral, but actually the fact that there were no sound or movement in them. I found the silence a little oppressive as we drifted during those periods of motor inaction, and was always eager to pull the cord and get going again. I knew that behind the leafed façades to the right and left monkeys sat, tree frogs clung, snakes coiled, lizards ran, birds perched and insects crawled—dozens of some, millions of others, all, during the daylight hours, quietly molten into their chosen backgrounds.

Only at night did this tropical forest give proof that its citizenry was not limited to plants. Gradually at dusk, then finally in the darkness, as we entered our hammocks, the jungle would awaken. Cicadas and crickets would begin sounding their shrill instruments; then gnats, midges and mosquitoes would cloud the riverside atmosphere to supply a softer fill-in tone; tree frogs, legions it would seem, let go with their own characteristic tympani effects; bats would appear but add no sound. Unseen were the nocturnal monkeys now astir, the rodents, the thousand other skittering things on branch, humus heap, log and water surface. Unseen too were the large ground mammals, among them the tiger and the tapir, starting out on their night wanderings.

The *tigre,* or South American jaguar, *Felis onca,* was once so abundant in these parts as to have been a very real threat to the raising of cattle and horses. Though weighing only 150-250 pounds, this carnivore is sure death to calves and colts, not to mention adults if young are not easily available. The tiger, whose yellowish coat is figured with black rosettes, is equally at home in jungle or open savanna: he is an excellent climber of trees, swimmer of streams and negotiator of tall grass. Except during a short sedentary period while tending kittens, he is a wanderer, a stealthy nocturnal prowler. He is known to have dragged a slain horse half a mile to the nearest water hole, the more fully to enjoy his meal; he is known to have attacked and killed a full-grown caiman. His traditional prey, however— at least in the more heavily wooded parts of the llanos—is the tapir.

I caught a glimpse of a tapir in the afternoon of the journey's second day, and the sight gave me a start, for this shy, semiaquatic mammal is not ordinarily found abroad during the daylight hours. We had rather abruptly come around a river bend when a queer, brownish-black creature about the size of a large hog ahead on a bank clearing suddenly lifted its long snout, peered in our direction for a second and then turned on stubby feet and plunged into the bush thicket. How this unprepossessing animal manages to survive in a hostile jungle is hard to say, for his eyesight is known to be bad, his body is big and tubby, his temperament nonaggressive. The tapir represents a very ancient hoofed form, once world-wide in distribution, now found only in Central and South America and in the Malayan area. He is of special evolutionary interest because he is presumed to resemble the mammalian stem from which both the modern horse and the African rhinoceros evolved. *Tapirus americanus* lives a very secretive life, mainly to avoid his arch enemy, the tiger.

How these two contrastive mammals first came to South America constitutes one of the most bizarre chapters in the book of paleontology. About seventy million years ago, when the Age of Mammals was just beginning, the continents of North and South America became separated by a water barrier where the Isthmus of Panama now stands. The fauna of the southern continent was in what the evolutionist calls a state of geographical isolation, and its mammals came to comprise one of the most unusual zoos ever known. Marsupials evolved in an abundance and diversity exceeded only by those of Australia. Queer, nearly toothless edentates flourished to produce eventually not only colossal ground sloths the size of modern elephants, but wondrously armored creatures with heavily spiked maces at the ends of their tails.

But even more extraordinary were the hoofed grazers and browsers that evolved and thrived during South America's Golden Age. One family, the toxodonts, looked like a cross between an enormous woodchuck and an Old World rhino; another family fairly resembled the modern horse; another, the camel; another, giant rodents; still another bore elephantlike tusks; and so on. These amazingly diverse ungulates were, of course, herbivorous. For reasons yet obscure, placental flesh eaters of the lion, tiger, wolf and bear types failed here in South America to evolve in parallel with the plant eaters. Consequently, for many millions of years the ungulates were free from the molestation of any dominant placental carnivores.

This was not so in the continent to the north, nor in Africa or Eurasia. These continents, interconnected by land bridges across the Bering Straits and the Red Sea, became populated not only with herbivores but with faunas of fierce feline, canine and ursine predators. Thus we may picture the western hemisphere of those days as consisting of two distinct and separated continents: the one to the north inhabited by both flesh eaters and plant eaters, the one to the south inhabited by a diversified mammal population which included, along with marsupials and edentates, an abundance of relatively guileless ungulates, but no placental carnivores.

Such was the situation when, in comparatively recent times (that is to say, somewhat more than a million years ago, for paleontology deals in approximations rather than in precisely measurable time units), the Isthmus of Panama rose out of the sea to create a land bridge connecting the previously disjoined northern and southern continents. Immediately and relentlessly the forces of animal migration went into play, and the handiwork of animal evolution moved in both directions across the intercontinental bridge. The southbound traffic consisted not only of competition-toughened herbivores (horses, tapirs, deer, llamas), but of wolves, saber-tooth tigers, jaguar and pumalike cats —an army of hungry newcomers, all drawn by the figurative smell of fresh pastures and easy meat. Few South American ungulates, during their millions of years of relative freedom from competition and molestation, had had experience with such creatures; they were unprepared to stand up against the competitors and killers pouring in from the north. And almost overnight, as geological time goes, the southern continent's bizarre spectrum of ungulates was virtually extinguished. The whole story may never be known, but from the inferential evidence there seems little doubt but that some sort of cause-and-effect relation existed between this invasion and this extinction.

As a bit of sardonic if not poetic justice, the invading saber-tooth tiger—too specialized, it is thought, to compete successfully for food once the less nimble species on which he preyed had been killed off—himself eventually became extinct, probably along with many another similarly over-specialized invader. But not so with certain species of cats unburdened with such exaggerated dental weapons; presumably faster, craftier and more supple, cats of the jaguar and puma variety could stalk prey elusive to the saber-tooth—and so were able to survive. Less easily explicable is the survival of the clumsy tapir, also among the Pleistocene invaders from North America.

In any case, today, some million years later, *el tigre* still burns bright in the forests and savannas of the llanos night. A descendant or derivative of big cat marauders from North America, he now lives scattered throughout the lowlands of South America to haunt and worry the equally enduring tapir or such other mammals as latter-day man has introduced.

I ducked as a bare branch hanging low over the water nearly brushed my hat off. As we passed under, I noted some handsome patches of lichen clinging to the bark.

Normally I should have reacted to the sight of a lichen with mild curiosity; perhaps I should have made an attempt to identify the species. But for the moment, that lichen, by now downriver fifty yards, struck me as representing quite the opposite of the fierce struggle elsewhere in the jungle, for a lichen comprises an alga species and a fungus species living together in what appears to be a state of happy altruism. The chlorophyll-bearing alga photosynthesizes atmospheric carbon dioxide and water to form nutritious carbohydrates which both the alga and fungus use as food. The fungus, for its part, supplies minerals for both partners, conserves moisture for both and gives skeletal rigidity to the union. This sort of harmonious living together in a world where carnivore and herbivore are words of inescapable meaning was impressive. Here the lichen appeared not solely as an example of symbiosis, which is how it is described in textbooks, but also and more significantly as an expression of the co-operative idea. Obviously the lichen relationship along with others of its kind does not involve any conscious social effort, but it is an indication that living things must not invariably destroy other living things in their efforts to survive. Here two species had joined forces in a benign union, each contributing to the other's welfare. I was about to construe all this as a sign that coexistent in nature with the competitive drive there may be a component analogous to the human being's capacity to function in accordance with the Golden Rule.

Then, as though to neutralize this slim hope, another of nature's altruisms came to mind—that practiced by the social insects. Think of the numerous ant species in which the individual is anatomically specialized to serve as warrior, or worker, consort, hive tender, slave supervisor; the species in which only one or a few individuals retain power to reproduce the appropriate number and kind of citizens to keep the society in balance and to serve in the capacity of queen-despot. Each such ant or bee colony is an internally rigid society in which freedom of the individual is almost wholly subordinated to the group purpose. This is surely social altruism, but operating within a framework of regimentation far exceeding in rigidity and ruthlessness any yet devised by man.

It is always risky to draw analogies between the behavior of the lower organisms and that of man. But can there be much doubt that human chromosomes are crammed with genes having the same evolutionary origin as the genes of any fierce tiger, mild tapir, regimented ant or benign lichen? A spectrum of the conflicting traits which comprise man's evolutionary heritage seems perennially to display itself in every individual's personal and social behavior. How to channel this contradictory jungle inheritance has constituted man's great moral and social problem ever since he began to fancy a difference between himself and the beast.

I was jarred from my musings not by the reproving image of Darwin but by an abrupt sputtering, then a stopping of the motor. My heart nearly stopped too. Without power behind it, the bow of the boat lurched downward, and we were adrift on the Arauca. Tomás, with paddle in hand, kept the boat in midstream away from the swirls and heavy overhanging branches near shore, while I grabbed the tool kit and went to work. Happily, the trouble was nothing more serious than a cracked spark plug which when replaced brought the motor back to life.

Later in the afternoon we turned out of the Arauca and

into the tributary Río Matillure; and in the morning of the next day (the third since leaving San Fernando) I caught a glimpse, through a break in the riverside vegetation, of a high English-style brick house standing on a dry-land elevation a half mile south of the river. This was Matapalos, a bit of Anglo-Saxony miraculously transplanted. Reputed to be the only two-story ranch house in all of Apure, it had been built, I learned, of bricks made from local clay and fired in improvised ovens. Separating it from our present position on the river was swampy grassland and minor jungle. We had scarcely two hours of fuel left in our containers.

Tomás pointed to a vague thinning in the shore grass. I slowed the boat toward this and turned off the motor. No sooner had Tomás dug in for his first pole stroke than with an enormous splash a crocodile or a caiman lunged out of the bank shallows about a yard from the side of the boat, then submerged quickly into the river depths. The creature's entire length had been briefly exposed, or at least about twelve feet of it. Three weeks earlier such an encounter would have been terrifying to me; now I joined Tomás in a little tired laughter. He said something I could not understand, but it might well have been, "Lo, the guardian of the Matapalos gate."

Tomás poled us into a narrow stream meandering through grass so tall that it obliterated my only half-believed view of the house. At length we came to a clearing where several dugouts lay banked, one with an outboard. This was the end of the voyage, a fact for which I was unutterably grateful, and I stepped out of the boat. A quarter mile of half-flooded meadow still separated us from our goal. Leaving the boat's load untouched, we set out across the shin-deep mud. We were about halfway there when I saw a man in rolled-up white trousers emerge from the house and start wading to meet us.

Tall, lean-faced, fortyish, Mr. John P. Kitson quietly took the envelope I offered him. Flying overhead were some wild ducks which had been feeding here until disturbed by us. Across the meadow stood three enormous jabiru storks looking gravely in our direction. And skittering about nervously on the acreage of algal scum, *Salvinia* weed, and lily pads were a number of pert jaçana birds with toes so long and so effectively splayed as to enable their owners to walk on the floating vegetation. The sun at this moment was streaming bright, and a pale-blue sky was aglow with massive cumuli. The setting contrasted paradisaically with the gloomy jungle-hemmed river environment of recent days.

When Kitson finished reading he turned to me and smiled. "Well, if it's birds you're after, I don't think you will be disappointed here. As to the scarlet ibis, these coro-coros, we may have to do a bit of looking." And we made our way toward the house.

In San Fernando I had heard almost legendary stories of the miracle of Matapalos. The house which Kitson and Briggs built far out in the remote llanos with, so to speak, their bare hands is considered throughout the Apure basin to be a world wonder. It stands there off the Matillure like something from another civilization, which in fact it is: brick walls, a big screen porch, proper hardwood floors, a staircase, a functional second-floor bathroom and three bedrooms. Only in the last named does one not forget that he is still in a primitive outpost, for bush hammocks hang where beds are expected. In the dining room is an icebox, and in the sitting porch is a short-wave radio tuned more or less continuously to the BBC's Latin American beam. Out behind, in a shed, is a big electric generator.

All this is possible because in summer the llanos muds dry up and trailered jeeps can haul in heavy supplies. Now, in the wet season, Matapalos is an isolated oasis to be reached only by a long river journey of the sort I had just completed. I sensed that Kitson was nearly as happy to see me as I was to see him; the flood season had been long and lonely. For a brief time I forgot all about coro-coros and reveled in the luxury of this place.

Kitson looked askance at my sodden sneakers and quickly supplied sandals of the sort worn universally in the llanos by peon and llanero alike. Then he showed me to a second-floor sleeping room. "Have a shower, then come down for lunch. I'll send a man to get your things from the boat." He left, and a few minutes later there was a knock. A clean, barefooted, olive-skinned peon girl of about twenty stood at the door with a tray on which, as in a magazine ad, stood a dewy bottle of beer and a sparkling glass.

Any hour of the day, Kitson was saying as he carved deeply into the breast of a roasted wild goose, his cook could send a boy with a shotgun out on the half-flooded meadow over which we had sloshed, and within minutes the hunter would return with the required number of ducks or geese. This was the land of birds. Had I seen any stink pheasants along the river? Kitson wondered with seeming irrelevance. These surely would be of interest to me, for their nestlings have claws on their wings, and they can crawl about like squirrels on the branches of the trees on which they are born. Kitson was referring to the hoatzin, which I did know as one of the strangest inhabitants of these parts. I wasn't sure if I had yet seen any, I replied, but did recall having noticed some pheasant-sized birds flying noisily, usually in early morning or toward evening, from the foliage of one side of the river across to the other. Did they screech? Kitson asked me. Yes, something like oilcloth being ripped. Kitson nodded: they were hoatzins all right. He would take me to some nests near by, if I were interested, and show me the clawed young.

I assured Kitson of my great and genuine interest in seeing baby hoatzins, but repeated that my primary ornithological goal here in the llanos was to find nesting coro-coros. I had by now recounted the Briggs and Bezara report. Kitson said that in a day or so he'd take me on a canoe trip upriver to the Bezara ranch, but agreed with Briggs that one look from the air would be worth a thousand rumors. He himself had not heard of that particular garcero, but was fully prepared to believe that one such existed somewhere along the Matillure, for (repeating the story I had heard so often before) in summer, red birds were always seen hereabouts wading in ponds along with egrets, herons and storks.

As to getting into the air, Kitson hesitated. He had been a flyer during the war and, as Briggs had said, did have a little plane which in the dry season he sometimes used for visiting San Fernando. Now, as I well knew, the ground everywhere in the llanos was soggy. He wasn't even sure his plane was currently in good repair. But after lunch we'd have a look. I was elated, of course, with the prospect of short-cutting my way to the presumed coro-coros, but ventured that, although finding those red birds was at this moment the most important thing in all the world to me, my own life came a close second.

It was actually not until the next day that we went to inspect the plane. Kitson had meanwhile sent some of his peons to trim the pasture grass. We pulled the little two-seater Cessna out from under its thatch-roofed hangar. One tire was nearly flat, so we went to work with a hand pump. But there was a hole in the casing through which an inner-tube bleb began slowly to protrude. We deflated, slipped a piece of leather into the hole, and pumped again. Probably hold all right, Kitson was saying to himself, unless we hit a sharp rock. Then he strolled out on the pasture. I saw him kick the sod a few times, as though to assure himself that it was as soggy as the half-inflated tire. Returning to where I stood next to the plane, he said that it was not the take-off but the first landing thump that was giving him pause.

But not too much pause, I observed, for Kitson now set about letting most of the air out of the other tire. Bring the inside pressure down to almost zero, and I don't think we'll have any trouble, he was saying to himself. Actually I did not think he was serious when he started pouring fuel into the gas tank, checking the oil, straining the struts and fins for stability. He started the motor, revved her a few times and beckoned me over.

"Want to try it?" he shouted above the motor's roar, smiling a smile that I did not know how to interpret.

Given time to consider, I am sure that I would have replied, "No, thanks. What do I want with coro-coros?" As it was, I impulsively piled in, fastened the seat belt, and we were taxiing toward the far end of the pasture. Kitson throttled the motor to full power and we began bouncing across the wet bumpy earth. Several times Kitson put his head out of the window and looked down at the tire. Each time he glanced at me and crossed his fingers in a significant gesture. Abruptly the bumping stopped as we slid into the air.

I saw the Matillure ribbon. The world there reminded me of that first sight I had got of the llanos the day of my aerial approach to San Fernando—patches of emerald foliage, half-scummed water expanses, a coiling river. I saw a herd of melancholy cattle standing in one stretch of shallows.

Previously Kitson had told me that he knew the location of at least a half-dozen garceros within a ten-mile radius of Matapalos. Perhaps one of these would have the ibis. The first we came to—a dense green patch of vegetation surrounded on all sides by flood—was whitened with egrets. We circled once—nothing red there—and went on. Then we came to a second foliage island which, like the other, had the appearance of recently having been snowed on. Here we circled again, with both Kitson and I craning our necks for a sign of scarlet. But only whiteness.

We were over what I think was the fourth garcero when Kitson suddenly nudged me, pointed down and banked abruptly. We had been flying at about 1,000 feet. He was lowering rapidly and circling hard. I saw perhaps a thousand white dots on the bushes there—then a daub of fifty or so red ones.

Chapter 5

EARLY NEXT MORNING we set out in Kitson's 22-horsepowered dugout, bent on making a preliminary examination of the marsh with the red dots. Kitson did not anticipate any particular difficulty in getting there, for, despite all the aerial circling and all the seeming distance covered, the garcero was probably no more than a few miles from Matapalos. From the air we had taken careful note of the *caños*, or channels, of the area; to get there we would have to push through some dense swamps and brush, but that would be no problem in a good heavy canoe.

We poled out along the grassy capillary which leads from the Matapalos meadow to the river. Then Kitson started the motor and, without comment, headed the dugout straight across the river and pierced it into the bank foliage of the other side, as though sticking a darning needle halfway into a coarse woolen blanket. Kitson suggested that I pull the vines and branches aside and crawl in as far as the bow had penetrated. A little mystified but not unwilling, I made my way forward, brushing aside impeding shrubbery. Then suddenly I stopped with the realization that a foreign eye was upon me. It was a curious eye, with a hard black pupil and gleaming red iris, the whole set in a patch of pastel-blue skin. There was something else new to me about that eye: lining the upper lid was a set of eyelashes so perfectly in place as to suggest their having been re-

140

cently mascaraed. The accompanying beak was much like
that of a chicken, but with a conspicuous nostril hole on
either side. Down below the eye, also located in the blue
skin patch, was another hole which I supposed to be the
ear opening or external auditory meatus. What added the
final peculiar touch to this already peculiar head was a
shock of feathers spiking up along the mid-scalp line, like
a Comanche tuft badly in need of combing.

The possessor of these features was otherwise hidden
from view, partly because of intervening leaves and
branches, partly because it was seated in a nest a little
above the level of my eyes. "What do you see?" Kitson
asked from his open-air position in the dugout's stern.

"A hoatzin," I whispered, "brooding on its nest." With
these hardly audible words I crawled forward, rising
slightly, thereby causing the brownish-gray bird to leap
vertically as if suddenly aware of something very hot underneath. Then, with a succession of quick, nervous hops
through the branches, the hoatzin broke out into flight over
the river. Kitson yelled something which, except for the
words *"chen-chena,"* I could not understand, for now the
bird was rasping in a voice suited to an enraged harpy.
The outcry decreased with distance and stopped abruptly
as the bird attained the green shelter of the Matillure's
opposite bank.

By this time I was close to the nest, looking into its loose
platform of twigs and grass. The three eggs there were a
little larger than a pigeon's, shaded a delicate pink and
blotched with several hues of brown and slate-gray. As
my eyes grew accustomed to the leafy twilight I discovered that there were two nests in this bush. One was
empty, its late occupants—several long-necked, half-naked,

mournfully ugly hoatzin young—perched near by. Two of these sat in a position normal to most birds, with toes tightly curled around a horizontal branch. A third, however, was clinging to one of the bush's vertical branches by means of a pair of claws on each wing.

Paleontology and comparative anatomy are usually presented only to those students in college who plan to go on into some specialized aspect of biology. It seems a pity that others are denied intimacy with these subjects, for they are basic to the understanding of evolution. In nearly every zoology textbook is a picture of *Archaeopteryx*, a fossil creature, half bird, half reptile, that lived during late Jurassic times some 100,000,000 years ago. Its celebrated imprint on stone, uncovered in 1872 not far from Solenhofen, Bavaria, remains today as one of the significant paleontological finds of all time. *Archaeopteryx* is presumed to represent an ancestral form which, in breaking away from the reptile line and growing feathers and taking to the air, became the evolutionary forebear of later birds. I recalled the picture of that fossil: the teeth (which present birds do not have), the feathers (which present reptiles do not have), the long vertebrated tail (missing in birds), the wings (missing in living reptiles), the claws at the tip of each elongate, feather-supporting finger bone.

My stare at that frightened young hoatzin clinging there was spanning 100,000 millennia. To be sure, these hoatzins had no teeth, no conspicuous tail; but their wing claws were evidence enough that somewhere in the family closet was the skeleton of a reptile. Although it is thought by some that the hoatzin's claws represent a secondary development, I seemed here to be looking at a vestige from a distant age, a living fossil. One wonders why the young hoatzin retained or developed this reptilian feature, or why birds in general do not have claws on their wings to augment leg claws as instruments for climbing or perching. Perhaps in most bird habitats wing claws would have little survival value.

Whatever the evolutionary explanation of their wing claws, these little hoatzin "lizards" were astonishing. And in ways other than as climbers. I reached forward very slowly to seize one of the yet unfledged creatures, but my intended victim suddenly released its hold on the branch and plummeted straight into the underlying swamp water. I kept my eye on the spot where the splash had occurred; nothing came up. Young hoatzins, using their wings as fins, are said to be skillful underwater swimmers, which is quite unusual considering that they belong to the Order Galliformes, a group including such nonswimmers as the pheasants, chickens, partridges, grouse, etc. My bird had no doubt swum submerged for a time, then quietly crawled up on a branch somewhere out of sight.

The hoatzin seems to enjoy an immunity to caribes, of which part of the explanation may lie in its common name, stink pheasant. Hoatzin body odor has been described as resembling that of a good ripe circus—straw, dung, peanuts and all. Kitson told me later that the bird's flesh is not very palatable; the only time a peon will touch chen-chena meat or eggs is for purposes of increasing sexual potency. The birds themselves are vegetarians, subsisting mainly on green leaves.

Back on the river, we set out again for the ibis marsh. The prospect should have excited me, and did; but I was so impressed by those hoatzins, which I had frequently read about but never seen, as to be diverted by thoughts of the days when creatures like *Archaeopteryx* dwelt on the earth. Furthermore, I was relaxed in the knowledge that my primary quarry was now safe; whether we arrived at the garcero today or the next day seemed unimportant. Kitson must have sensed my attitude, hence his interest in demonstrating the zoological curiosities along this llanos riverbank.

For a time nothing else of a spectacular nature presented itself: there was a small caiman or crocodile floating quietly near the mouth of a caño we passed, a green snake coiled asleep on an overhanging branch, a frog sitting on a log— sights commonplace to me at this advanced stage of my travels. Commonplace, that is, unless one should begin to reflect on the fact, mentioned earlier, that geological ages ago the evolutionary forebears of these respected and abundant llanos citizens were actually fishes.

From the beginning of vertebrate time to the present, the breathing tissues of fishes have been physiologically suited to absorb oxygen only from water. The breathing tissues of that caiman and snake, on the other hand, were designed physiologically to absorb oxygen only from air, while the frog has lungs at one stage of its life cycle (a reminder of its tie to higher air-breathing vertebrates) and gills at another (a reminder of its link with fishlike water-breathing forms). The facts of paleontology indicate that fishlike water-breathing creatures gave rise to the stem which produced the amphibians; from that stem grew a stem which produced the reptiles; from that stem grew two stems, one of which produced birds and the other, mammals.

But this spectacle of vertebrate synthesis could not have occurred except for at least one special event, an event without which I should not now have been looking for the scarlet ibis; indeed, without which I—that is, man—would not have been on this planet at all, nor would the scarlet ibis or hoatzin, the caiman or snake, or even the frog. That event involved the transition, rather the emergence, of vertebrates from a restricting habitat of water to one of air and land—in terms of anatomy and physiology, the replacement of gills with lungs.

Of course, no fish ever stood up in a swamp and walked out on dry land in testimony that he had suddenly become terrestrial. The process, beginning more than 300 million years ago, occurred at an incomprehensibly slow rate, one advantageous mutation presumably adding to the next, to produce finally a creature capable of back-and-forth life between water and land—in short, an amphibian. All this is thought to have transpired in an ecological system which, reminiscent of these very llanos of Venezuela, was subject to seasonal flood and drought, or in an ecological system undergoing a slow change from the character of a swamp to the character of a desert.

Whenever there was a drought in those days, the water of shrinking swamps would sooner or later become depleted of oxygen or fouled by the action of putrefactive microorganisms. Fish inhabitants would perish, either from suffocation or poisoning—that is, all except those that had developed an internal membranous sac connected to the throat by some type of bronchial duct. In the earliest of such deviants, this sac was probably no more than a simple tissue pocket which, when its possessor came to the surface and gulped, would fill with air. The oxygen contained in that gulp of air would diffuse into the walls of the sac and so be picked up by the blood stream. Functioning as a primitive lung, the structure presumably gave its owner a slight survival advantage over other fish whenever the oxygen content of any shrinking pool dropped below that needed for gill respiration. By the process of selection during thousands of ensuing generations, this innovation was improved on, the sac progressively developing into a bi-lobed "lung" whose interior became crinkled and otherwise adapted more efficiently to the absorption of atmospheric oxygen. But these air-sac lungs had yet a long way to go before they would enable their owners to stay out of water indefinitely, their original purpose supposedly having been only to augment the gills during times of water deoxygenation or fouling.

Today, only three remnant species of lungfishes survive, all inhabiting lands where flood alternates with drought. One species is found in Australia, one in Africa and another in South America. At the approach of the dry season the contemporaneous lungfish burrows into the muddy bottom of its shrinking pool, while the solely gilled fishes fall victim to predators or die from suffocation. Imprisoned thus in a muddy coating lined with waterproof slime, the lungfish goes into a form of hibernation, drawing air into its lungs through a pore or crack in the mud. Six months later when the rains come and the muds soften and the pools and rivers are re-established, the creature awakens and returns to its previous life in water, breathing now and again by means of surface gulps.

About the time that air sacs were developing in some fish species, certain others were undergoing changes which resulted in the formation of lobed, as distinguished from finned, appendages. These lobes, four in number and ventrally placed, were supported by bone arrangements comparable in basic design to the limb bones of present-day amphibians. Eventually a combination of such locomotive and air-breathing equipment occurred to produce a preamphibian capable of gulping air and also of lumbering across moist land. That creature, providing two essential keys to terrestrial living, left the water—presumably not for feeding purposes (for Devonian pools must have been stocked plentifully with edible things), nor for oxygen (for by merely coming to the surface it could gulp all the air it wanted), nor apparently to escape enemies. Paradoxically, it became a land animal while making an effort to remain in the water.

Conjure up the picture of a vast Devonian swamp abounding in all manner of fishes. A drought comes; waters recede until there remain only separated pools and lagoons, each packed with trapped fish. In the smallest of the pools the oxygen eventually is depleted; fouling results, and all individuals dependent solely on gills or skin absorption for breathing die. Any fish possessing a structural arrangement for gulping air, together with a capacity for crawling, has a chance to escape to a neighboring pool which may be deeper and perhaps not yet threatened by total evaporation. The adventurous fish sets out across the land bridge, the while staying alive by gasping air and swallowing it to fill the rudimentary lungs. The first fishes to do this successfully became the planet's first amphibians —paleontologically known as labyrinthodonts, now long extinct. They somewhat resembled present-day newts and salamanders but were larger, some the size of crocodiles.

That the amphibians never became a dominant animal group is probably due to the fact that their challenge of the land was only halfhearted—indeed, no true challenge at all. To this day frogs, toads, salamanders, newts live mainly in moist habitats, lay unshelled eggs and have young which, like fish, breathe by means of gills. They never got beyond the stage of swallowing air, as distinguished from drawing it in by means of an expanding thorax; nor did they develop a hide impervious enough to prevent water evaporation, a lethal handicap in any hot, dry climate.

But with the caiman and snake—with reptiles—it was another story. Except for secondary regressions back to the water, reptiles became wholly terrestrial, developing watertight skins and a thoracic system for inhaling and exhaling. So equipped, they radiated into nearly every variety of the earth's many and ever-changing environments. Just as the fishes were the dominant vertebrates during much of the Paleozoic era, so, spectacularly, were the reptiles during the Mesozoic era extending from 200 million to about 65 million years ago. Feet and lungs they inherited from amphibians; but not reproductive habits. The production of shell-covered eggs was an exclusive reptilian contribution to vertebrate evolution.

Just as the wheel was critical to the development of human mechanization, so may the development of the covered egg have been critical to the emancipation of vertebrates from the restricting ties of water. The apparent discoverer of this secret was an advanced amphibian-soon-to-become-reptile, typified by *Seymouria,* a long-extinct genus named after the town in Texas near which its fossil bones were discovered. Due to each ovum being provided with enough nutrient yolk material to feed the embryo during its period of early development, and then the whole being plastered around with a tough membrane, eggs were produced which would not quickly desiccate when deposited on dry land and which therefore could safely be cached away wherever the bearer chose. Animals that could produce such eggs became the planet's first true land vertebrates, and a foundation was established for evolution along lines never before possible.

It should be noted that the egg layers did not, however, in a literal sense abandon water; they merely learned how to convert it to private use. The embryo of every reptile, bird and mammal has its own lagoon; for whether encased in a membranous or calcareous shell or, as occurred later, implanted in the wall of a uterus, there is an amnion, or bag of waters, in which the growing embryo rests suspended. By this means, terrestrial vertebrates have avoided the amphibian necessity for depositing their eggs in an open aqueous medium and for being consequently forever subject to the chance of drought.

Descendants of those first egg layers came to be the great armored stegosaurs, the flying pterosaurs, the giant 50-ton brachiosaurs, the herbivorous and carnivorous dinosaurs and a thousand other "Lost World" nightmares. Some reptiles continued to crawl in quadrupedal fashion like their amphibian forebears; others rose on their hind legs to introduce bipedal running as an interesting new form of vertebrate locomotion; some, developing membranous wings, took to the air; some even returned to the water to become aquatic or at least amphibious again. Of all these mighty monsters, only turtles, snakes, crocodiles, lizards and tuataras remain today. Somewhere in that jumble of Mesozoic reptiles arose the mammals, standing by to take their turn as masters.

It was actually before the Age of Reptiles had begun

that certain curious lizardlike animals evolved whose anatomical features sufficiently overlapped those of later mammals to win for their possessors the paleontological position as originators of the mammalian line. Such half-reptile, half-mammal creatures were very common in the Permian and Triassic periods, but with the coming of the Jurassic and Cretaceous, and the overwhelming dominance of true reptiles, they underwent a mysterious eclipse. What prevented their extermination during that 150 million years of reptile dominance could very well be related to their not having become rigidly adapted to any particular environment. It was such very rigidity, presumably, that led to the downfall of the great reptiles, for with geological and ecological changes occurring on this planet at a rate faster than creatures of high specialization could keep up with or accommodate to, dinosaurs, brachiosaurs and their kind fell massively by the wayside.

Of course the picture of those days is a fragmentary one. Fossils tell only the story of bone anatomy and give little hint as to whether the premammals were, for example, warm-blooded, had hair, were equipped for nursing their young, etc. It is believed, however, that in many ways they resembled a small opossum. Just when or why such forms abandoned egg laying and started to bear their young alive is a moot question, for fossils, again, rarely record the morphology of soft parts.

Inferentially suggestive in this regard are two groups of primitive mammals living today: the first lays eggs, just as reptiles do, but engages in a type of nursing; the second comprises the marsupials. The spiny anteater, as an example of the first group whose only other member is the platypus, incubates its leathery-shelled eggs in a maternal

Next morning early we set out in Kitson's 22-horse-powered dugout, bent on making a preliminary examination of the marsh with the red dots.

The author and his aides at Algarrobito.

A peon family, and assorted guests, wait for their supper.

Any hour of the day one could go out across the flooded meadow at Matapalos, and within minutes bag the required number of ducks or geese for the table.

Kitson amuses himself with a snake found sleeping on the roadway at Matapalos.

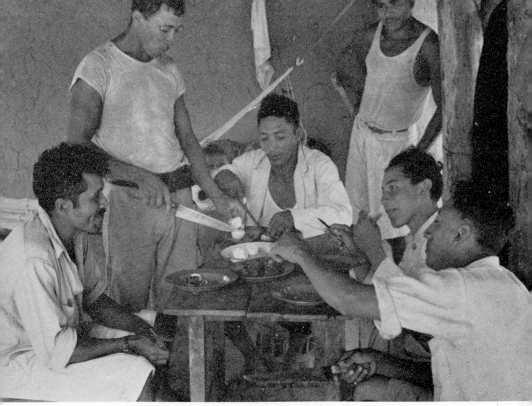

Mealtime in a llanos hut.

At camp, the author repairs his monkscloth birdblind.

The polesman leads us into a dusky world of face-slapping leaves and trailing lianas.

skin fold. Upon hatching, the young get nourishment by licking up a secretion elaborated by certain modified glands in the mother's skin. True nipples are absent, perhaps because the mouth parts of the young are hard and unsuited to the suckling process. Marsupials, on the other hand, typified by the kangaroo, bandicoot, wombat and koala bear, do not lay eggs, but retain their embryos in the body until the latter attain at least the fetus stage. So premature are such young when born that they cannot even exert enough muscular effort to suckle. Accordingly, the lips of each helpless fetus become affixed to a teat, and milk is pumped in by means of muscular exertion on the part of the mother. At a later stage the young marsupial releases its hold on the teat and suckles in the voluntary manner of higher mammalian young.

But many additional changes had to take place before an adequate platform came to exist on which the Class Mammalia could be constructed. In the reptilian egg there is a membrane which lies very close to the inner surface of the shell. This membrane, the allantois, is serried with capillaries which during incubation provide surface for the exchange of respiratory gases between the embryo's blood and the outside atmosphere.

Advancing mammals, having rejected both the shelled egg and the pouch, evolved a system for retaining within the mother's body both the fertilized ovum or ova and the ensuing embryos. The allantoic membrane now became embedded in the mother's uterine wall, where its blood capillaries mingled intimately with those of the mother so that feeding and other physiological exchanges could take place between mother and unborn young. With the mother as a specific food source, the need for large stores of yolk material, characteristic of reptile and bird eggs, was obviated.

But mammals differ from their reptilian precursors not only in mode of reproduction. There are, obviously, a host of other physiological and anatomical divergences: mammals have hair, sweat glands, two sets of differentiated teeth, a muscular diaphragm, two skull joints, marrowed bones, improved kidneys, a closed four-chambered heart, warm blood, a system for maintaining internal body temperature at a high and constant level, a larger brain, a generally speeded-up metabolism and hence a more alert life action.

It is difficult to say which of these, or of unlisted others, was the key character leading to mammalian dominance, although one might guess that the adoption of high internal body temperature and its thermostatic control was as important as any. Thus the mammalian body, inside, is always operating at tropical temperatures, whereas the lower vertebrates (except birds) must adopt the temperature of the surrounding medium and consequently become subject to climate variation in a very literal sense. The internal metabolism of a desert Bedouin goes on at precisely the same temperature as that of an Eskimo; likewise with a seal in the Arctic and one swimming in tepid tropical waters. It is not difficult to see how this sort of thermal control would have an enormous survival value. During cold weather most amphibians and reptiles become metabolically sluggish and are thereby easy prey for an active enemy; on the other hand, any animal of high metabolic temperature sustains its alertness regardless of climate. The physiological mechanism for controlling internal temperature too may have kept early mammals from overheating or freezing during certain geological periods when great areas of the planet's surface became exceedingly hot or cold.

Mammalian success, whatever its mainspring, may be seen as radiating into nearly every environment of this planet: the bat in the air, the whale in the sea, the camel on the desert, the tiger in the jungle, the simian in the tree, the goat on the mountainside, the bison on the plain, the mole in the ground. Man, the most magnificently adaptive and resourceful mammal of them all, has reached the point of recognizing no environmental barrier. The land is his, and the sea and the air; and space will no doubt eventually be his. Someday the mysteries of the inner environment too may yield.

Kitson had turned the boat into the heavily foliaged mouth of a small tributary flowing into the Matillure from the north. Because of roots, grass and shallowing water, the motor soon became more hindrance than help, and we maneuvered the dugout manually by tugging on lateral or overhanging vegetation. After half an hour or so of such laborious travel, we moved out of the shadows into a sky-lighted world where jungle foliage thinned into an open flood plain; the horizon was clear except for some not too distant heaps of low shrubbery. Kitson pointed to an area perhaps a half mile off where the heaps were covered with the familiar whiteness of egrets. We started the motor again, intending to circle the garcero rather than to proceed directly to it. All at once a reddish dot on one bush there caught my eye. I glanced at Kitson; he saw and nodded and immediately turned off the motor. We both picked up paddles and with cautious, quiet strokes slowly eased the boat in the direction of the colored bird.

Before very long we were between and among the white-powdered bushes. The egrets were relatively indifferent to our presence; only that single red bird standing atop his otherwise apparently deserted bush seemed to sense our preoccupation. Suddenly, with a furious fanning of wings, the bird leaped up, streaked rapidly through the air and disappeared beyond some higher bushes in the background. A split second later about a dozen more red birds just like him churned up out of the same bush, followed by about ten more from an adjoining thicket. These too were gone before I had time to take a second breath.

But I was sure. Those beaks—long, thin and curved-down—together with the flight manner, were the identifying features. I had finally come upon *Guara rubra* in its true natural state. As for the elation expected in anyone about to attain a long-sought goal, there was an element of dubiety and delay: the redness of these birds had little in common with "dazzling beauty"; nor had they in flight borne much resemblance to "flaming" jets.

What peculiar mockery! I thought. After months of nourishing the belief that the scarlet ibis in the wild would be something of matchless quality, I found these specimens chromatically not much more interesting than bricks. In fact, they were no more exciting than the egrets all around, or the anhingas and herons and storks I had become accustomed to during all my weeks of llanos searching. To be sure, the birds had appeared colorful from the plane, and they were certainly redder and sleeker than those specimens in the Bronx Park Zoo or the coop at San Fernando; but they did not even vaguely correspond to the published accounts nor to my lavish mental concept. I brooded sadly but said nothing.

Kitson had maneuvered the canoe alongside the bush where we had first seen the single ibis and was busy pulling branches aside and looking in and through toward the center of the thicket. "You know," he was saying, "I think those were immature birds. See, there are no nests here." At this I hastily joined him in thoroughly examining the ibis bush, also the other bush that had yielded red birds. Only excrement stains on the branches, green scum on the water below—no sign whatever of nesting activity. "No use chasing those birds," Kitson continued, pointing in the direction the ibises had disappeared. "The coro-coros I've seen many times in summer are bigger and much redder. I should have noticed that from the air the other day. These are the same birds all right, but this is no coro-coro garcero. These bushes are just roosting spots for last year's young."

Kitson pondered a moment, then added, "We could go up in the plane again. But frankly, I think it would be wiser for us to make a trip to Bezara's place and look into that story Briggs and Rafael told you in San Fernando. Some peon at Bezara's might very well, without fuss or bother, be able to take us straight to a garcero of nesting coro-coros."

Accordingly, next day we pulled up at the Bezara mudbank. We had used my boat rather than Kitson's, because in open water it was faster. The sound of the approaching motor had attracted several peons, who in curiosity accompanied us up to a sprawling, low-built ranch house with a windmill in back that seemed oddly out of context this time of year. Neither of the Bezara brothers had yet returned from San Fernando, so we were received by the foreman. He asked us in for coffee, and we were shown mildewed snapshots of one of the Bezara tiger hunts. Kitson, of course, spoke fluent Spanish and was entirely at home with these people. The foreman listened attentively to Kitson's explanation of my visit and to the Bezara coro-coro story. I could get only snatches of the conversation. Finally the two stood up and I followed suit in what had become to me a well-worn procedure. "Do we have enough gas for another two hours upriver?" Kitson asked me. "The peon Rafael had in mind lives at Algarrobito." I had filled several of my reserve tanks at Matapalos.

The foreman decided to join us; so, with the boat now overweighted, the trip to the next settlement was slowed somewhat. Otherwise all went well, and by two in the afternoon we were at the riverbank metropolis of Algarrobito, which consisted of one cow path, two thatched huts and a visible population of one woman, several men and two small children. Here again we sat, drank coffee and inquired. Kitson translated: "The man we want is visiting at a hut we passed a half-mile downstream."

Thirty minutes later we found our man asleep in a hammock. Awakened, he said without a second's hesitation that, yes, certainly he knew where there were coro-coros, thousands of them; and he pointed vaguely in an upriver direction. I was not impressed. I had learned, alas, that a thousand years is as a day to many of these people, and so with their coro-coro arithmetic. The man strapped on his holstered knife and sandals and joined us on the return to Algarrobito, where we transferred the outboard to what appeared to be the village dugout, a boat certainly more suitable than mine for swamp penetration and for carrying passengers now numbering five.

A short while after setting out upriver we turned into a typical thicket-hidden caño so narrow and entangled that again hand tugging or poling came to be the substitute for propeller power. Finally, as on the previous afternoon, we broke out into a more or less open flood plain, rich in grass and green with scum. Methodically the second peon whom we had asked along for this purpose ascended to the very tip of the dugout's bow and began poling. He would plunge his pole into the hip-deep water; then, pushing the hand end of the pole before him, he would lunge and run down the length of the unoccupied forward half of the 20-foot-long canoe, which yielded each time with a powerful spurt ahead. We cut through long lonely stretches of prairie seas, across hyacinth-patched lagoons, into wildernesses of grass, up squirming channels where the water was often swift.

Sometimes as we entered an area of high grass, mosquitoes would cloud up and for a time make life a misery. And it was these rather than the swamp that put me in mind again of the planet's earlier days, diverting me somewhat from the miseries and disappointments I felt were at hand. In Carboniferous times ferns towered up sixty feet, and club mosses grew to be as high as eight-story buildings. Insects and other nonbackboned animals swarmed through that awesome vegetation. The oldest insect fossil comes from Silurian rocks, almost 400 million years old. Cockroaches, mayflies and dragonflies seem to have been the most abundant insect types in Paleozoic swamps, or at least were the ones most effectively fossilized.

There were probably no mosquitoes as we know them. But the great swamps of the Carboniferous had an insect population far more spectacular than that of any llanos swamp. In those days dragonflies had a wingspread of two feet, and mayflies were almost as large. I have said that the flood-drought pattern is thought to have been mainly responsible for the emergence of vertebrate life from water to land. But the early amphibians conceivably would never have survived on land if the air and vegetation had not swarmed with succulent insects and larvae. Amphibians today are still mainly insect eaters.

However, with mosquitoes droning all around, I had little inclination to credit the lowly insect as responsible for all vertebrate evolution. Indeed, practical thoughts on the subject of malaria now seemed more appropriate. Many of these llanos mosquitoes, I was quite aware, were Anopheles, and thereby suspect of bearing the disease. But my awareness of this was more or less academic, for I knew that it is mainly mosquitoes encountered in the villages and around river hovels that are dangerous. Since my arrival in San Fernando I had each day taken a double dose of Chloroquin. Furthermore, I knew that the chances of a malaria-carrying species of Anopheles out here in this flooded grassy plain being itself infected with a variety of malaria causing the disease in human beings were remote. There is a prevalent idea that any mosquito which in biting extends its abdomen vertically into the air is sure to transmit malaria. The truth of the matter is that an Anopheles capable of transmitting the disease to the human body must first have qualified in a precise and difficult series of events: it must be a female and must have drawn blood from a person in the so-called gametocyte stage of the disease; and about ten days must thereafter have elapsed while the malarial cells, now in the mosquito's body, undergo their various maturing cycles. Only then is the mosquito able to transmit the disease. Accordingly, I could with almost absolute certainty assume that the mosquitoes clouding up out of the grass and drawing blood from our skins were uninfected with the organisms which produce malaria in human beings. And even had they been, my Chloroquin-saturated blood stream would have offered no suitable environment for the malaria organism.

While my thoughts on mosquitoes were definite and reassuring, those on the subject of bird finding were at this juncture somewhat mixed and confused. From my llanos experience to date, I had come to the point of believing that anyone who said he could show me coro-coros was, prima facie, a dealer in fractional truths. Yet, admittedly, only 24 hours before, I had seen living young of the species, whose elders must exist somewhere. Rationally, I had no reason whatever to doubt the peon's claim; experientially, I was full of misgivings.

We had had no rain that afternoon, although the sky had continuously been masked by a low, sultry, steel-gray overcast. It was about four o'clock when Kitson, after some talk with the guide, pointed to a line of foliage on the western horizon: "The garcero's supposed to be beyond that *monte*." This supposition received some support when, as we approached to within about a half mile of the foliage wall designated as a *monte*, I began slowly to be aware of bird life in the air somewhat beyond it. Some of the moving dots came from the north; many more streamed in from the southeast; all seemed to converge on an area of common rendezvous. The birds were yet too far away to be seen as anything but silhouettes.

Then abruptly, flying directly over us, at an elevation of no more than fifty feet, streaked four jets of scarlet— bright, rich, magnificent scarlet. They were aligned one behind the other; black coal flicked at the tip of each flaming wing. In a few seconds they were out of sight beyond the foliage barrier. Kitson's eyes had been on them too. "That the kind of coro-coro you're looking for?" he asked casually.

We were now at the foliage wall, looking for an entrance. Here the tangle was formidable, and we made some false starts before finding a spot thin enough to pierce; at that, it took a considerable amount of bushwhacking on the part of our crew before we could get the canoe in. It was gloomy, nearly dark, in that dank vegetation; wet leaves brushed across our arms and faces, and thorns and spikes threatened on every branch. But the barrier was less than fifty yards deep, and soon we burst forth again into the open. The guide immediately stood up and pointed southward where the watery horizon was broken only by foliage heaps of the sort Kitson and I had seen elsewhere the day before. "*Los coro-coros*" was all the peon said.

The first bush I saw, about an eighth of a mile away, was covered with birds of dusky hue. Beyond that was another bush—no, a great assemblage of bushes, some hemispherical, some shapeless, some flattened close to the water, some rising twenty or thirty feet into the air. They were all "as if spattered with blood."

Chapter 6

BECAUSE of the nearness of night, we could remain in the Venice of the scarlet ibis only long enough to confirm that this was not a wishful dream. Almost hurriedly we turned out of the swamp, retraced our course across the flood, back to the guides' huts at Algarrobito. Darkness was already with us as Kitson and I transferred the outboard to my boat and set out on the return trip to Matapalos. In retrospect that journey seems like a halloween ride, but there was no moon to show us the way. Kitson sat high in the bow of the little boat, somehow managing, through the blackness and occasional showers, to shout or semaphore navigational directions to me at the tiller. I was a devil released on that downstream course. For three solid hours, except during brief impatient times out for refueling, I kept the throttle wide open, roaring around the curves, sweeping through overhanging bank foliage, gleefully jerking the stick this way or that to avoid such inconsiderations as sandbanks and floating logs. My indifference to hazard sprang, I suppose, from an airy exuberance produced by the afternoon's magnificent climax. I was heading back to Matapalos to take Kitson home, and there to provision myself for a protracted period at the garcero.

Accordingly, three days later I found myself again in a world of scarlet birds. There was no sun that morning.

The air, characteristically, was dank, and the sky was heavy with rain clouds. A violation of reflection optics as I fancied I understood them, the water of the garcero shone a luminescent green instead of reflecting the sky's somber quality. Against the soft attentiveness of the vast bird congregation and against the backdrop of gray clouds and stubbornly green water, I witnessed bush after bush consume itself in fire as the canoe approached and passed. After each eruption there remained a heap of ashes, for the verdure of the garcero vegetation had long since been dimmed and grayed by bird droppings.

Adding to the garcero's reverence-inspiring aura was a great outdoor silence—the silence of the deep swamp. The voice of the scarlet ibis can hardly be heard, and even in a state of frightened alarm it is feeble. Except for the whir of feathers beating against air, there was very little audible here. Absent conspicuously from this garcero was the cacophony of screeching egrets and herons.

Birds generally have a higher metabolism than other animals. Avian blood is richly oxygenated, in contrast to that of the more sluggish reptiles (excepting the Crocodilia), whose peculiar heart structure permits the main arterial stream to be thinned with energy-depleted venous blood. The high-gear setting of their nervous system seems reflected in the lightning reaction time and the abrupt muscular movement of most birds. Vision and hearing are exceedingly sharp. Body temperature exceeds that of most animals, heartbeat is more rapid, digestive efficiency far greater. In short, most birds physiologically and sensorially are attuned to a life of racing speed. Yet this seems like an understatement, as I recall the sight of those some eight to ten thousand scarlet ibises on this my second visit to the garcero.

Very often, the closer we got to a bush, the redder it became, due to the sudden pouring of alarmed ibises from their nests within to the periphery. Then, in the take-off there was no gradual acceleration such as I had seen many times in a Caribbean flamingo rookery. This was a species that let go with the reaction time of exploding dynamite. It seemed as if the bushes were wired so that each would detonate in direct and constant proportion to our distance away. Straight up into the air—each scarlet mass would be cohesive for a second or two, then dissipate as its components leveled off and sped in every direction.

In formal philosophy, matter is usually regarded as having three primary and basic qualities: the first involves space, time, shape, motion; the second involves such sensory reactions on the part of the observer as color, taste, sound, etc.; the third has to do with beauty, which is an indefinable factor. Here in the garcero there were shape and motion aplenty; there were flamboyant color and, though hushed, sound; there was beauty that I am unable to define or adequately to describe, or even to deny that it reflected anything more than perhaps my own willing sense of wonderment. Yet, recalling the words of others privileged to have been among scarlet ibises, I feel that the beauty of these birds was not solely a function of my own personal aesthetic susceptibilities.

The garcero covered too large an area of the flooded plain to be viewed in panorama from any one spot. In general, it consisted of about a hundred variously sized, mostly thorned, acacialike bushes spaced irregularly, each as an

entity rising out of the water. A few of them lifted themselves up ten or fifteen feet, but most were not much higher
than the eye level of a man standing in a dugout. The water
was uniformly about three feet deep, suitable for easy poling, and barely but implacably flowing southward in a great
horizon-to-horizon sheet, eventually to be shoved out into
the Matillure channel.

By now deep into the garcero, our boat was drawn up
close to one of the huge nesting bushes. There were temporarily no birds on it; but from a distance it had stood out
deeply reddened and so had been selected as an adequate
target for our experimental blind operations. There were
only three of us on this second visit: I, and the two peons
from Algarrobito whom I had engaged to double as dugout
crew and field staff. Manuel, in whose hut I had set up my
field headquarters, was undersized, wiry, sharp of face;
Ventura, who occupied the other hut at Algarrobito, was
taller, strongly muscular and had a mobile face and sense
of humor that were easily touched off. In the complexions of
both men shone a dark walnut mixture of Spanish, African
and Indian pigments, characteristic of so many a llanos
peon.

These men seemed to understand that my motive for
returning to the garcero was to observe the coro-coros up
close; but why I was at this moment driving a wooden
stake into the gluey swamp bottom must have puzzled
them. My command of provincial Spanish had not yet improved to the point where I could offer a full explanation.
Without Kitson to translate, I had been depending more
on my hands than on my tongue, and my hands were very
much occupied with the stake. I had instructed Manuel,
in the narrow bow, to hold onto the branches of the bush

so as to prevent the boat from moving out from under me as I worked. Ventura, studying my motions with some perplexity, stood by in the stern. The feathered inhabitants of the near-by nesting bush had, of course, long since flown to the safety of other bushes fifty or sixty feet away, on whose tops they were perched, watching us. All closer vegetation was deserted, due to our invading presence.

I had uprooted a sapling at Algarrobito which, now trimmed as a stake, extended above the water's surface about two feet and seemed solid as a wharf piling. I caught Ventura's eye and pointed to a spot near the motor where lay a tool kit containing a screwdriver, wrenches, an oil can, spark plugs, etc., together with a pair of pliers and some bailing wire. While he worked to disentangle the wire from the jumble in the kit, I reached down under a tarpaulin spread ostensibly to protect the cargo from rain and extracted a folded beach umbrella. Manuel's job during these activities was to keep hanging onto the bush and, insofar as possible, to stabilize the boat.

I had seen no sign nor heard mention of caimans or caribes. And since the water here was no more than hip-deep, I grew bold and started pulling off my trousers preparatory to going overboard. The task of affixing the umbrella pole upright to the stake could be expedited immeasurably from a working position in the water. I had removed one trouser leg and was pulling the second down over my foot when suddenly, as the meaning of this action dawned on my observers, their respectful silence was replaced by streaming and excited talk. Ventura, in a voice colored with apprehension, his hands pointing simultaneously at the water and at my bare legs, cried, "No, no, señor! *Muy peligroso!*" He continued with great animation to read me some sort of riot act, to which Manuel added his own frantic volleys of confirmation. I did not understand much of what was being said, but the word *caribe* was enough to reveal the general idea. I hastily drew my trousers back on and was grateful to proceed as before, grateful also to escape the mosquitoes and flies that had immediately landed on my bared legs.

Holding the umbrella stick in close juxtaposition with the vertical stake, I was able finally to wind bailing wire around the two, then to twist it tight with the pliers. When enough loops of wire had been wound around and the poles were one, I laid aside the pliers and opened the umbrella, then made my way back into the stern of the dugout to view the thing in proper perspective. What I beheld looked about as ridiculous as anything possibly could. There in the middle of fairyland stood a big six-feet-across hemisphere of garishly striped canvas—an escapee, it appeared to me, from the clutter of Miami Beach—that sheltered absolutely nothing but a pack of hypothetical caribes. But most innovations tend to startle until they are tested and found worthy, and with this in mind I proceeded to phases two and three of the day's program.

Amidships of the canoe, packed in along with sundry other items of cargo, was a small table. Any guilt I might have felt for borrowing it from Manuel's hut that morning was assuaged by the knowledge that in due time I would return it, together with a suitable rental fee. The woman who lived with Manuel had displayed no concern whatever as we carted off her one and only eating surface. I had previously given her two lipsticks picked up at a variety store in San Fernando, and they far outweighed the temporary inconvenience of a tableless home. She did not even object when, the night before, I had nailed 12-inch-long extensions to each of the table's four legs. Not that this table was a piece of Chippendale; it consisted of a rough wooden top somewhat less than two feet square, with four unfinished lengths of 2 x 2s to serve as legs.

There it sat, upside down, in the canoe. Getting it into place, topside up under the umbrella, was the problem. I asked Manuel and Ventura to help me lift it, which they obligingly did amid much rocking of the boat. We got the thing into the air, and then heaved it feet first into the water next to the pole. It was easy, although the ibises in the nearest occupied bush construed the splash as a signal to be off. The length of the nailed-on leg extensions was perfect. Their ends now rested on the bottom, and the table surface cleared the water by a good six inches. I placed a wooden grocery box on the table to serve as a perch for my bird watching. I was pleased. But the structure still required proving, so I stepped out over the gunwales, onto the table top and, not without some creative satisfaction, sat myself down on the box. It was sheltered and pleasant there under the umbrella, and the box, as boxes go, was comfortable.

At that moment a flow of Spanish language again broke into the quiet of the garcero, the combined voices of Manuel and Ventura suddenly rising to the pitch of excitement. I was vaguely aware of more scarlet ibises taking off somewhere to my left. Manuel was gesticulating wildly and Ventura was furiously wielding a paddle in an effort to swing the heavy waterlogged canoe back alongside the table from where during the commotion it had been allowed to drift.

It was only then that I became aware of certain dynamic

changes occurring immediately below me. At a slow but very sure rate I seemed to be moving in the general direction of China. I hastily looked over the side of the table and saw that what had been a six-inch clearance between garcero and table top was now only a three-inch clearance, then a two and finally a one. Ventura was too flustered to be very effective with his paddling; the boat at its present rate would not be alongside for at least ten seconds.

Under my weight the table legs continued to sink into the swamp's gooey bottom, and already garcero water was beginning to break over the tops of my sandals. Thoroughly scared, I made a lightning calculation as to the distance between me and the slowly approaching side of the canoe. I could make it in three plunging leaps through the waist-deep caribe water.

Now the water was nearly up to my ankles. At that moment, Ventura managed to get in a few very deep and telling side strokes with his paddle, and the canoe eased alongside. But (alas for a dramatic rescue) at that very instant the table stopped sinking. With one hand on the welcome gunwale, I wiggled with a downward pressure on the box, testing, and stamped my feet on the table top a few times. The table legs were definitely on the garcero's hard pan, or at least firmly stuck in the mud. And caribes would certainly not venture into the shallow water that lapped at my ankles.

I grinned, continuing to sit there, but the other two recovered at a slower rate. Finally, when convinced that the table would sink no farther and that caribes would not rise to attack my feet, the men resumed a more placid acceptance of the situation. Synchronously a cloud of ibises settled on the bush recently vacated, sixty feet away.

I stepped back into the canoe and unpacked a large circular piece of monk's cloth, which we flung over the umbrella top. It extended downward on all sides, nearly but not quite to the water. A little readjustment was needed so that the peepholes were at the right height— and the blind was ready for use.

With no loss of time, I lifted an edge of the cloth, maneuvered myself from the safety of the dugout and back onto the flooded table top. Arranging myself on the box, I instructed my helpers to paddle off about a quarter of a mile and to leave me for a trial session of bird watching. Then I lowered the curtain. I was alone now; the world could not see me, but I could see it. Eagerly I put my eye to the peephole facing the bush.

There before me, rising out of the water, was an entanglement of heavily thorned and sparsely leafed branches. A wise location for a nest, I thought. What marauder could possibly negotiate those spikes? The position of my blind seemed equally well chosen, for almost within arm's reach, as though someone had considerately placed them there for me to examine, were three nests, each containing a couple of eggs. Although appearing to be but tenuously attached, I later found that the twigs and reeds comprising these nests were tightly woven in and around tough underlying branches. The eggs, a little smaller than pullet eggs, were light brown, with dark splotches scattered over the surface, maximally on the blunt end. There was no fuzz or down; these next-generation scarlet-ibis ova lay uncushioned and uncomfortable-looking on their mats of crude sticks.

My eyes focused more deeply into the bush, and I saw

that it was crowded with nests. In every available crotch, on every available branch platform, was a heap of whorling twigs, some with eggs, some without. Those without, I surmised, had already hatched their season's brood, a surmise confirmed a little later when I shifted my position and spied out of one of the blind's other peepholes. There, a considerable distance away but near enough to be studied, was a large bush in the upper reaches of which perched a hundred or more immature ibises whose size and behavior indicated that they had but recently left their nests. During the blind-building operations they had shared the garcero's general concern and crawled deep into the foliage. Now with the disturbance over, they had returned to their surface positions.

These young were distinguished from their elders by a conspicuous lack of scarlet plumage, most of the under feathers being white, the wings, back and neck dusky. They could flutter awkwardly from branch to branch; some were able to fly short distances. Every few minutes a single adult scarlet ibis, presumably arriving from feeding grounds remote to the garcero, appeared in the air above and, with big commotion and gaudy show of pinions, landed amid the group. The hungry youngsters would seethe with anticipation, plunging their heads forward in curious beckoning gestures.

The actual feeding operation was so rapid that careful observation of it was next to impossible. An immature bird would dart its beak into the adult's mouth and almost instantly withdraw it, gulping. Then others would try to do likewise, until the adult, wearied or empty, would fly off. Whether the parent bird recognized and fed its own young or whether the feeding was indiscriminate and communal, I was unable to determine.

I returned to the first-used peephole, hoping that by this time perhaps some of the parents would have ventured back to their nests. But no, they had not, and their eggs seemed even more disconsolate than before. Watching from the safe distance of another bush, they had yet to overcome their distrust of the blind. But I knew from earlier experience that all birds will eventually consider a blind to be part of their normal environment and will come to show complete disdain for its presence. The observer must patiently wait for the birds' memory to dim.

While so engaged, I saw first signs of life in the bush. Deep down where the branches arched out of the garcero waters appeared an immature ibis slowly making its way, stepping awkwardly upward. Apparently this young bird, deserted by its parents at the time of our arrival, had not been able to join them in their flight to safety. It had taken the next best defense measure and retired deep into the protective density of the bush. Later observations confirmed that its brothers and sisters living in the same bush had been a little ahead in development and, although not yet finished fliers, could at the sign of danger at least flutter to another of the garcero's bushes.

The poor waif continued the ascent. Perhaps its memory was shorter or less practiced than that of those watching from the security of the distant shrub. Perhaps it thought that the men had gone and that the blind was now harmless. I watched and noted how the bird-child's feet were too big for its body and how its unkempt gray-and-white plumage gave no hint whatever of the superb coloration of adulthood. Finally, achieving the top of the bush, the bird now stood in the open, hoping no doubt that its parents and its young bushmates would soon return.

Then death came suddenly. I have seen it happen to bulls in an arena, to rabbits in a field, to a caterpillar under the sole of a shoe and to people in an automobile. But at no time has the sight of violent death overwhelmed me with more philosophic a bitterness than on that morning there in the garcero, otherwise tremulant with life. Why the destruction of an insignificant young ibis should have affected me in such a manner I am unable to say. An evil-looking caracara hawk, with its serpentine head, its viciously hooked beak, its icy eyes and its mercilessly taloned feet, became the symbol of death. With silent and unannounced vehemence it had descended on the ibis, had dug in its talons with one quick agonizing squeeze, and then as quickly had flown off, carrying the limp corpse.

For a time I stared at the now ibisless twig on top of the bush. Why must living things undergo death—some violently, some placidly, some in youth, some in old age, but all finally? That ibis a short while before had held a destiny of beauty, was possessed of an avian consciousness. By this time the creature, well shredded, was no doubt undergoing protein digestion in the bowels of the hawk. What had become of that destiny, that avian consciousness? Had the hawk's death-dealing action rendered everything about the ibis extinct? And inescapably, what happens when a man dies?

Thoughts on death's meaning have afflicted man since the beginning. Wonderingly, perplexed, he has seen animals die, has watched himself pass away generation after generation. Even as far back as neolithic times, believing that death is not the end, man buried weapons and travel accouterment with his dead. Later the human creature came to see himself as a dual entity composed of mortal body and immortal soul. The phenomenon of human life was construed by some as a spiritual test trip between two eternities. In beliefs ranging from nirvanic foreverness to literal resurrection, man has never ceased dreaming, hoping and praying that death is an exit, not a terminus. Yet no one denies that at least biological death is inevitably the lot of every living creature.

The biologist can supply no clue as to the meaning of death in terms of the individual's consciousness and spirit; but in terms of evolution he can. Let the story—not a pretty one—begin when life on this planet consisted mainly of single cells or fragments of protoplasm clinging to wet surfaces or floating free in the primordial waters. If I had had a microscope with me in the blind, I could easily have found more or less direct descendants of those one-celled ancestors of us all living and abounding in the garcero waters. Then, as now, such organisms lived either on ambient chemicals in the water or on energy supplied by the sun and were not subject to death from old age. As single cells, they grew until reaching a fixed size limit, then split in two, leaving no parent—and no corpse. In a sense, they were immortal.

In the course of evolutionary time, organisms developed consisting of many cells, the vast majority of which—relegated to serve supportive or nutritive functions—were shorn of their original capacity to reproduce the entire organism. Further division of labor occurred; and as millions of years rolled on, the cellular constituency of the advancing organism became highly diverse and astronomically large. Some internal tissues served to digest food for the entire organism; others were specialized to deliver nutrient to every cranny of the body; still others were assigned to impulse transmission, to locomotion, excretion, protection. But ever secluded and sheltered within each organism were the precious germinal cells, waiting. The whole "aim" and "purpose" of the outer body had become one of nurturing and protecting the select sex cells and of depositing them, when ripe, for fusion with those of another individual.

The time span allotted for this mission—that is, the period from birth to senescence—is gene-determined for each species. A tiny animal called the rotifer completes its entire life cycle within a few days, and during this period, having passed on its undying germ cells, then itself dies; the mouse does not age and die until one or two years of reproductivity have elapsed; some reptiles live to exceed a hundred and fifty years.

In life's two-billion-year reaction chain, no value was assigned to postreproductive maintenance of the individual organism. The diversity and adaptability of evolving species were enhanced by this generation-to-generation scheme, this life-death-life-death pattern, since, in the mixing of hereditary factors during fertilization, offspring differing from either parent were produced. Those individuals whose constitutions enabled them to cope with the planet's endless ecological shifts, or to radiate into more favorable environments, tended to survive and to pass their valuable new gene combinations into the main stream of the species' germ plasm. Thus survival of the evolving species, not of the single being, was the pre-eminent goal in animal evolution. The institution of death arose as a result of this null value placed on the individual once it had passed on its packet of genes.

As the hawk-ibis incident attests, not all, indeed very few, individuals realize their full life span, which for most mammals is calculated to be about six times the period from birth to maturity. The nature of the competitive biological milieu is such that predation, mishap, nutritional deficiency, failure of a vital organ or system, or invasion by predatory microbes or other parasites, usually terminates life long before true old age and natural death set in. In man, such factors have these days become considerably minimized, making the "sere and yellow leaf" stage all the more conspicuous. But in the end, the hawk comes. And where does consciousness go then, and the accumulated inner energies of a lifetime? The biologist has no hint to the answer.

To contemplate a bit further on the hawk's summary action against the young ibis, what of the factor of violence so deeply embedded in most animals, including man? To be sure, there must have been much jostling and pushing on the part of the planet's earliest quasi-motile cells as they sought to absorb nutritional chemicals from the waters in which they lived, or, when they had become photosynthetic, to get into the beams of energy-bearing sunlight. But there was little specific effort on the part of one individual to destroy another—no preying, no life living on death.

As evolution progressed, many organisms abandoned sunlight or ambient chemicals as a source of primary energy. At this crucial point these—the animals—began to prey on one another or on plants for sustenance. And there appeared progressively in the planet's jungles, plains, waters and forests an incredible array of horns, claws, talons, teeth, beaks, fangs, poison glands, stings, and finely integrated nervous systems with which to direct the use of these weapons. Defensive structures developed in parallel or in step-wise fashion.

One recalls in human history how the spear defeated the club, how the arrow defeated the spear, how the musket defeated the arrow—right down to the present hydrogen bomb and its obsoletizing effect. Most nations of the earth are armed, as though they themselves were organisms; or, if not armed, they are at least in the "protective" sphere of some nation that is. The survival motive, and the willingness to inflict violence in order to survive, seems to be nearly as much a part of human nature as of the tiger's.

Higher plants, having chosen the sedentary way of life, developed but few means or weapons for predation or violence. There was no need to, since green plants continued to secure their vital sustenance directly from sunlight. The only aggression to be found among most such organisms is of the same sort exhibited by the earliest algae—struggle for optimal light or struggle for optimal water or soil chemicals. "Violence" among the higher, as well as among the lower, plants consists mainly of crowding and pushing. One sees dogwood crowding out some of the lowlier plants in the field, or weeds competing for the soil in which the lawn should grow. This struggle, even though it does involve starvation and death for some of the competitors, is only circumstantial and positional.

Although I had been sitting there in the blind for a full hour, not a single scarlet ibis had ventured back to those nests. Perhaps *Guara rubra* was a shrewder species than I had supposed. Perhaps the birds were remembering that a man had entered the blind but that none had yet left it. Or perhaps the hawk had scared them away. In any case, I decided to give them a chance to forget and get accustomed to the garcero's new edifice. I would call it a day and return to my quarters at Algarrobito.

I drew up a corner of the monk's cloth, preparing to shout for the men to come fetch me. Then I got a surprise that served well to drive thoughts of death and speculative biology hurriedly from my mind. There, with its bow not more than ten feet away from the blind, in plain and conspicuous sight of every inhabitant of the garcero, was the dugout firmly tied to a root stump with its occupants sitting quiet and still as two graven images. Naturally no scarlet ibises had returned to my bush while the entire male population of Algarrobito had remained exposed behind my blind; it was evident that Manuel and Ventura had never left the spot. I felt frustrated but not angry, for it was clear that these men still distrusted the table structure and, in my interest, had elected to stay close. They could not have entirely understood the purpose of the blind; to them it may have been as reasonable for me to have set it up as a protection against sun and rain, as for an instrument of deception.

Trying not to reveal my disappointment, I expressed gratitude and indicated that I was through for the day. Quickly the canoe was untied and I was retrieved from my box-and-table quarters. We would leave the blind exactly as it was, thus not only allowing the birds to get accustomed to its presence but also to give it a 24-hour test against the elements. If next day we found the structure secure, I felt certain that Manuel and Ventura would see fit to leave me alone in it.

That the presence of an occupied canoe close to the bush was indeed the cause of the birds' failure to return quickly became evident as we poled away. We were not more than 200 feet from the bush when at least a hundred adults and fledglings swarmed in and instantly garnished it. One gleaming adult even landed on the umbrella top before hopping down into the foliage.

As we moved on, en route to the flooded meadows and thickets that lay between us and the Matillure, it was not distance that first blotted out sight of the garcero, but rain. For some time I had been hearing muffled thunder. Now close lightning produced flashes of eerie whitening over the garcero. Then the rain began, and the world of red disappeared completely behind a watery curtain.

At Algarrobito the lady whose table I had appropriated personally delivered to my hammock a bowl containing a whole boiled chicken. The broth was unseasoned and insipid, and on it floated a distasteful layer of yellow fat. But my hunger prevailed, and I tore off a leg and set to. Manuel and Ventura were served boiled beef. Why I had been favored with fowl (a comparative delicacy in this land of beef eaters) was perhaps suggested by my hostess's lips, which since I had last seen them had become as scarlet as the birds among which I had been all morning.

The storm had passed, and with the coming of evening I wandered out into the neighboring pasture, where next to a tree I located a spot with enough grass to cover the mud. I sat down to watch the sunset, but even here could not escape the world of birds. Although we were some miles from the garcero, Algarrobito seemed to be directly under an air corridor leading from the garcero to an ibis feeding grounds somewhere in the less flooded lands to the southeast. Through this corridor were now flying home-ward-bound scarlet ibises. It was the end of their day and should have been the end of mine. But I lingered; the sight overhead was one I had almost despaired of ever seeing.

The flocks above me, flying at altitudes of some one to three hundred feet, varied in size from a few individuals to several score, and in form from straight or undulating Indian file to amorphous bunches. Some groups were spear-headed, like geese in flight—although scarlet ibises do not seem to be as geometrically minded as geese, for often a few individuals would be out of position, giving the eche-lons a ragged appearance.

But compensation for this indifference to line symmetry lay in the rare hues and tints assumed by the birds as they swept over. Responsible to a considerable extent for this chromatic richness was the high component of red wave lengths in the sunlight of evening, and also my angle of view. Flocks approaching from the southeast, flying into the sun, would at a distance be colorless gray, then sud-denly pink. Speeding nearer and overhead, they would undergo a whole series of spectacular color shifts, through pink, rose, dark red, to flaming scarlet, finally as black silhouettes disappearing garceroward.

I wondered how these birds knew exactly where the garcero lay. But after a moment's thought I realized that their homeward flight required no extraordinary naviga-tional powers. When Kitson and I had been in the air a week earlier over similar terrain, we had found our way by simple visual means—cues provided by the character

of the twisting river, by conspicuous islands of vegetation
on the flooded horizon, by the position of land elevations
here and there. Furthermore, it is probable that at 300 feet
these birds could actually see the garcero or at least the
swarm over it. They hardly needed more than good eyesight to get from nests to feeding grounds and back.

The scarlet-ibis foraging area extended all the way from
the Matillure to the Arauca, where the land was less deeply
flooded than around the garcero. What the birds found to
eat there is conjectural. White ibises of our Southern states
feed mainly on small crustacea, worms, larvae, etc., which
with their forcepslike beaks they extract from mud or soft
soil. When subsequently I examined the stomach contents
of several adult scarlet ibises and found only green plant
material, I concluded that at least those individuals were
living on a diet of green shoots, grasses, etc. Yet I doubt
that such botanicals are the permanent and exclusive food
of llanos ibises. Later I presented Kitson in Matapalos with
an immature specimen taken from the garcero. The bird
became completely tame and would eat greedily of almost
anything offered. Manuel told me that more than once in
summer he had seen scarlet ibises boldly following newly
opened plow furrows in search of worms.

In December, when the dry season begins, the garcero suddenly evaporates and the nesting bushes become
vacant and lifeless. During this period the entire region
shrivels; bottoms of former swamps turn into cracked mud.
Most of the ibises will scatter far and wide in a search for
food—throughout the entire Orinoco basin wherever ponds
and lagoons and soft meadows remain, even as far north
as the coast and the delta swamps. At the time of this dispersion, the new generation of ibises is fully fledged, al-

though still in drab and colorless uniforms. They will not begin their transition to the plumage. of adulthood for many months and will not attain full redcoat status for nearly three years.

In May and June, after six months of wandering, the adults, along with sudden rain and rising waters, will return to the garcero with their scarlet pigments more radiant than at any other time of the year. As though drawn by a magnet suddenly and powerfully energized, the ibises come in from all directions, using charts still unfathomed by ornithologists. Mating time has come, and not only does love laugh at locksmiths; it laughs at problems of bird navigation.

Other bird species too perform incredible feats in this regard. How, for example, do some birds manage to fly thousands of miles to the tropics in the fall, and then in spring go back not only to their old territory in the north but actually to a particular barn, nesting tree, or pond? How do sea birds, experimentally carried inland over terrain they have never seen, return, when released, in a seeming beeline, through fog, rain and clouds, to their home island far out to sea? How are the proverbial exploits of homing pigeons accomplished? Landmarks, orientation to the sun, cues based on the earth's rotational movement, sensitivity to the earth's magnetic lines, inborn memory pattern of ancestral migration routes, extrasensory perception—each of these has been suggested as pertinent to the facts of bird navigation, but none has been widely or exclusively accepted. How birds on long journeys make their way through space is almost as much a mystery now as in the days of raven-fed Elijah.

As I sat with my eyes skyward, the sun was beginning

to sink into the horizon, and a splintering diadem of orange and yellow streamed up through western cloud banks. Cruising swiftly and without sound through these melting heavens came one scarlet-ibis formation after another. I had no way of gauging the actual speed of these birds, but, considering that wild ducks normally cruise at about fifty miles an hour and sparrows at thirty, I guessed that the flying flames above me were doing about forty-five. Using my wrist watch as a timer, I crudely clocked the rate of wing flapping and got an average of about four beats per second—fast, but not when compared to the humming-bird's more than fifty strokes per second, or the sparrow's thirteen strokes, or even the duck's nine. But whereas a modest four per second was the cruising wing beat of the scarlet ibis, their emergency rate is something else again, as evidenced by the ibises I had watched earlier in the afternoon exploding from their nest bushes.

How the institution of flight originated in evolution is not known. There were flying reptiles 150 million years ago, but they had no feathers, employing instead a skin membrane stretched on either side of the body between the torso and a greatly elongated digit bone, not unlike the system used by present-day bats. The best relic example of this sort of primordial flier is *Rhamphorhynchus,* an early Jurassic reptile about a yard long, with a fiercely toothed mouth and a thin tail with a lobe at its tip to serve as a rudder. This creature, like those anhingas in Chico's garcero, was a fisher and able to negotiate both air and water. But *Rhamphorhynchus* left no surviving descend-ants. *Archaeopteryx* is the oldest known bird fossil, which, if its feathers had not imprinted themselves on that Ba-varian stone ages ago, would, on the basis of just its bones, probably have been classified as a small reptile rather than as a transitional bridge between scaled reptiles and feathered birds. *Archaeopteryx* may have arisen from a line of bipedal arboreal reptiles which, living in forests, developed proficiency first in hopping and gliding among the branches. In Cretaceous rocks the remains of other bird types have been found, but on the whole the early fossil record of birds is meager.

However, there can be no doubt that somewhere along the way an offshoot from the reptile stem developed certain skin structures never before seen on animals of this planet: horny, keratinous elevations destined eventually to become feathers. Nothing is known of the initial purpose or function of these hypothetical structures, if any; for, again, there are no fossils to show stages intermediate between scales and feathers. But whereas the genesis of such prefeather innovations may be obscure, the occurrence of true feathers in reptiles of the *Archaeopteryx* variety is unchallengeable, as is the fact that feathered flight eventually became an authentic and persistent mode of biological travel. The feathery covering developed by birds served also to conserve body heat, to streamline against air resistance, to repel water, etc.

But it was not alone the development of feathers that made flight possible. It was a whole series of other anatomical and physiological revisions as well. Bones had to become hollow and lightweight; sternum structures had to fuse into a solid keel on which powerful wing muscles could be attached; lungs had to send little fingerlike sacs throughout the body so that flight muscles could be more directly oxygenated, and also so that pumping would automatically serve as an aid to inhalation and exhalation; circulation and metabolism had to be geared to a life of speed and alertness.

With the utilization of the fore appendages as wings, birds (the hoatzin being one of the few aberrant exceptions) forever lost the use of them as tactile instruments. But for this loss nature had an answer. From a mechanical point of view one would think that the head, housing as it does the brain as well as three principal sense organs, would be about the last part of the body to be selected as a seizing, tearing and probing instrument. Yet, as it happens, the bird head, via its beak, has come to be used in just that way. One need think only of the raptorial beak of the hawk, the mud-digging shovel of the duck, the piercing spike of the anhinga, the nut-cracking vise of the parrot, the pile-driving tool of the woodpecker and the ordinary hunt-and-peck beak of the chicken to see how birds compensated for their loss of hands and fingers.

The sun had by now gone down, the sky had burned itself out, and the ibis procession had dwindled to a few stragglers. I got up from where I had been sitting under the tree, yawned and started walking back toward the hut. Then suddenly I quickened my pace as I became aware of small shadowy fliers closely overhead. I recalled Kitson having mentioned the relative abundance of vampire bats in the llanos—how the horse disease *murrina* is carried by them; how he had found animals, the morning after a serious attack, with withers a bleeding mess, blood still leaking down over the forelegs. Of course I knew perfectly well that vampires will not molest a moving man, that they do not hover over their intended victims like mesmerists in helicopters, neither do they seek out the neck and jugular vein, as Dracula-indoctrinated people sometimes suppose. A toe sticking out of a hammock is a more likely attraction. The incision made by a vampire results not from a single bite but from multiple scrapings inflicted by the bat's razor-sharp teeth. The vampire does not suck blood, but laps it up as it flows to fill the little tissue crater so produced.

With such rather gruesome thoughts passing through my mind, it did not take long for me to reach the hut and to enter my hammock. Two other hammocks, hanging close and parallel to mine, bulged heavily with the bodies of my sleeping hosts. I quickly pulled my zipper shut, checking carefully to see that it was closed all the way. Now three hammocks bulged in the quiet bat-flecked llanos night.

Chapter 7

NEXT MORNING we found the covered umbrella and its sheltered table exactly as we had left them. Manuel and Ventura seemed reasonably convinced of my future safety within the monk's cloth cell, and no sooner had I disappeared into it than they obediently poled away. That this time they were really out of disturbance range was confirmed in what seemed to be only a matter of minutes, when through the forward peephole I saw an approaching red streak suddenly materialize into a perched object of stunning splendor. There, on a branch no more than four feet away and framed by the raveled edges of the crudely cut hole, was *Guara rubra*, a portrait in glowing scarlet.

Considering all the threats to life, limb and sanity I had endured for the privilege of this moment, I should, after a short interval of fervent thanksgiving, have rejoiced in getting down to the serious business, first, of observing and recording ornithological data and, second, of taking pictures. As to the latter, I had not brought my photographic equipment along from Algarrobito, pending further testing of the blind. As to the former, if I were a proper kind of field ornithologist, the remainder of this chapter might well consist of a complete and annotated description of every move, nod and gesture not only of the radiant creature nearly within arm's reach but of the other birds that had now begun to shower down upon the bush. To record such

186

details of bird life is certainly a justified aspect of natural history, and worthy men have spent lifetimes at it. In addition to using blinds, binoculars, collecting and preserving equipment, calipers, scalpels and statistics, they have rigged nests with delicate temperature and movement recording devices so as to obtain information on the many variables of bird home life. How long does each parent sit on the eggs before being relieved? At what temperature are the eggs incubated, and how does it vary through the day and night? How much time is needed to complete the relief ritual? How much egg rolling is there, what is its pattern, and so on?

The reader who yearns for information of this sort about the scarlet ibis will find me a rather dismal ornithological failure. I had come to the llanos equipped only with a camera and, alas, a somewhat straying point of view regarding birds and nature.

Regarding the specimen seen through the peephole, I was interested to note the absence of whatever droll appearance had been displayed by those semidomesticated birds in San Fernando and New York, notwithstanding the fact that the beak of this garcero bird bore the same preposterous relationship to the body as it did among those in captivity. The caricature aspect of the zoo inmates was replaced here with one of imposing dignity—often an attribute of those who have not suffered transplantation.

I wondered why this bird stood there so idly, so detached. Was he still suspicious of the blind, or had he no eggs or young to tend, no mate to be relieved? I was quite sure that apprehension was no factor, for elsewhere near by there was now a continuous coming and going of birds. I finally concluded that either he was inexplicably a bachelor or, more likely, that he had lost his mate sometime earlier in the season. And although he would not by nature's dictates rewed until the following season, his gregarious instinct appeared to bind him unbreakably to the colony.

As to "his" sex, the male and female scarlet ibis are externally indistinguishable—a condition common to such marsh birds as the egret, heron, roseate spoonbill, flamingo. Why the sexes in some bird species look identical, not so in others, is undetermined. Although there are many exceptions, advanced dissimilarity seems to be correlated —via either cause or effect—with the solitary nesting habit, similarity with the colonial nesting habit. When the sexes appear to be dissimilar, the drab female often takes on full domestic responsibility, while the resplendent male struts and poses; when they appear to be similar, nest care is usually shared by both parents. Whatever the significance of sexual similarity in *G. rubra*, the specimen now in view, male or female, was one of nature's loveliest conceptions.

While thus showering dignity and color on the scarlet ibis, nature seems to have been reluctant in the bestowal of weapons. The bird's beak was blunt, its toenails were unsharpened, and its eyes had a gentle, soft, bambi quality. *Guara rubra* could well be used along with the dove as a symbol of peace. I thought again of that hawk, with its fierce talons and ripping beak, and wondered how the scarlet ibis had managed to survive at all, with its pacific nature and its screaming color.

And what color! The Kodachrome reproduction included in this book has a devious history. In the garcero, light reflected from the bird was gathered by the camera lens and focused to strike a sensitive film emulsion. On later processing, this film was treated so that it would differentially soak up certain primary dyes, including red. By projecting more light through the resulting Kodachrome transparency, photoengravings were made on metal by a chemical etching process. These plates were smeared with colored inks, which in the printing press were transferred to a paper sheet.

What the reader sees in the frontispiece bears only limited correspondence to what I saw that day through the blind peephole, with the light reflected from the bird striking my retinal tissues directly. The quality of light falling on the reader's eye as he looks at the color reproduction is obviously something quite different. When I compare what I see here now and what I saw there in the garcero, I realize (without in any sense libeling the engraver, who did as good a job as modern technology would allow him) how inaccurate and inadequate photography really is.

I once had a professor who, in reaction to the old saw that a photograph never lies, said that a photograph always lies. I did not at the time understand what he meant, rather uncharitably dismissing the remark as that of a pedant trying to impress his class with some brand of iconoclasm. What he may have had in mind is now clear to me. Every phenomenon and experience in life has a nearly infinite number of aspects. A man becomes aware of these to the extent that the native acuity and breadth of his senses and perceptual faculties will permit. The camera has but two senses, those of line and light; only these can be recorded in any picture, which, accordingly, must be incomplete and, to this degree, inaccurate.

In this connection one might despair over the trend in modern life to depict nearly everything photographically, as in the illustrated newspapers, the mammoth picture weeklies and monthlies, even in the home snapshot album. By getting so much of their information from photographs these days, men have come to lean on a few oversimplified and easily comprehended dimensions for their day-to-day enlightenment. Pictures, whether on neolithic cave walls, in the Louvre, on a movie or television screen or in the pages of a magazine or book, have always been attractive because of their ease of comprehension and the amount of precise information apparently there. But even when sound and movement are added, any picture constitutes only a few-dimensional aspect of a multi-dimensional phenomenon. In recent years the printing press and the various visual-projection techniques have made pictures a dominant institution for mass communication and learning. One wonders if this tendency to feed on something that "always lies" may not be one of the sins of our times.

Yes, the color reproduction in this book reveals some aspects of the scarlet ibis, and the text comprises an additional dimension or two. But no man who has not himself been in the midst of a garcero with all his senses stirring will know the beauty of the scarlet ibis.

And even now, late in October with the nesting season almost over, I doubt that I was seeing the ultimate in scarlet ibises. Maximum sheen and elegance of any seasonal bird is sustained only during the earlier phases of the breeding period—in the case of the llanos scarlet ibis, May and June. The exuberance of mating, nest building, the daily flights to foraging grounds, brooding—all these take a toll in feather-tip injury and breakage, irreparable until after the postseasonal molt. An unfair human parallel would involve the comparison of a person's appearance during courtship with the same after domesticity has set in.

The evening before at Algarrobito I had been impressed with the effect of varying light values on bird coloration. Here now in the blind I was also aware of this. Earlier the sun had briefly shone on my specimen, but now the garcero's illumination was indirect and subdued, due to the blanket of clouds lying between earth and sun. So filtered, the light tended to be relatively meager in warm tones, abundant in the so-called cold tones. Anything green looked greener; anything blue looked bluer; but anything red was slightly dulled. Scarlet ibises are not maximally red unless observed in direct sunlight, and not glorified except in early morning or late afternoon when the light is predominantly warm. Human complexions look rosier in the morning or evening; likewise the pigments of red birds.

Again now, the sun came out, and my bird was transformed into a blaze of scarlet. I looked at my watch; it was not quite eight. We had left Algarrobito before dawn.

Animal coloration is usually regarded as serving a function in courtship, or in concealment, or warning, or species recognition. The purpose of color in the scarlet ibis would not seem readily to fall into any of at least the first three of these classes. Since both sexes in the scarlet-ibis species are externally identical, their color would hardly be of value in courtship. The birds are so conspicuous that, at least to the color-visioned human eye, concealment could be no factor, although the possibility of the scarlet ibis having natural enemies who are blind to red cannot be ruled out. As to warning, the color red has for us as human beings a universal meaning, but whether red would have a similar connotation to enemies of the gentle ibis is questionable. That the color of the scarlet ibis functions at least to some extent in species recognition was indicated by an incident I observed that day from the blind.

On a bush not far away was a nest with a brooding ibis of snowy white, indifferent, it seemed, to her status as ugly duckling in an otherwise nearly pure community of scarlet birds. She was obviously a *Guara alba,* common in the South American tropics as well as in our own Southern states. *Guara rubra,* comprising the only other species of the genus *Guara,* is limited in occurrence to the coast and littoral of eastern and northern South America, and of course was the overwhelmingly predominant citizen of this garcero. Anatomists have never been able to find a single structural difference between the two species: they have exactly the same bones, claws, feather arrangements, beaks, and other features used ordinarily to establish the taxonomic position of birds. Only in feather pigment do they ostensibly differ. Some authorities, accordingly, have wondered whether the white and scarlet birds are but color variants and not separate species at all.

I kept vigil on the white bird. Would the mate—presumably away at the feeding grounds—be white or scarlet? If white, the indication would be fairly strong that color had been the cue to recognition, and furthermore that *Guara alba* is genetically a distinct species. If red, it would seem that the color as a recognition aid was negligible and no valid character to serve as a basis for placing the red and the white birds in separate species, for a species, by definition, is a group that in nature freely interbreeds.

For a long time nothing happened. The mates of other near-by nests came, engaged in egg nudgings and odd sorts of ceremonials, and thereupon replaced their partners at brooding. Then suddenly a white he or she appeared from above and landed on the bush, making a total now of two stark-white birds there among the some fifty scarlet ones. The bird hopped over close to the nest, crossed beaks a few times with the brooder and seemed generally happy to have come home. With no great pomp or circumstance, the latter rose, gave the eggs a few farewell nudges, then yielded the throne position. The newly arrived bird checked the state of the charges, rolled them a bit more with the end of his beak, and then with an uplift and ruffling of feathers proceeded, like a crinolined lady sitting down, to settle for a session of brooding. The other bird was already gone, heading Algarrobito-ward.

White to white, scarlet to scarlet—that appeared to be the recognition and mating story of the genus *Guara,* based on this and subsequent observations from the blind. So far as I am concerned *alba* and *rubra* may continue to be classified as distinct species, a classification that they themselves apparently respect.

It had not previously occurred to me that the presence of brooders and egg clutches here this late in the season was somewhat anachronistic. Indeed, nowhere throughout the garcero was I able to find a single nest with recent young; all had eggs or were empty. The many preflight immatures (I later estimated them to total at least several thousand) indicated a rather high percentage of successful families earlier in the season. It seemed that any attempt at this late date to produce an additional brood was fore-doomed, for within a few weeks the rains would stop, the floods would go, the feeding meadows would dry, and the garcero would abruptly cease to be. Such late-October activity was a valiant though blindly instinctual effort to produce an additional family before the inevitable dry weather drove off adults and fledged young in a dispersed search for food. Tragically, the effort could end only in wholesale death to eggs and to whatever hatchlings might remain in the nests when the signal for dispersion came. Animals have a tenacious fidelity to their immediate young, but the impulse to live and reproduce yet another day seems to come first. Manuel told me that in past years he had visited the garcero just after the December break-up to find forsaken eggs in almost every nest, or dead or dying infants. Ten thousand birds require a lot of food and will quickly exhaust the unreplenished store of any withering meadow.

In view of the inevitable destruction awaiting these eggs, I had no conscience later that day in cracking open a number of them. I poured the contents of each into a drinking cup for close examination. In some, riding high on the yolk mass, was a little red disk no larger than a pinhead—a 48-hour ibis, scarlet not from feather pigment but from haemoglobin. In others, more advanced, I could see blood-filled vessels reaching out in all directions from the primary embryo, like the leafless branches of a winter tree. The four little stumps I saw on some of the larger embryo bodies would one day have become legs and wings.

Earlier, each of these half-formed creatures had been but a single microscopic ovum extruded from the mother's ovary, and soon thereafter fertilized by one of the millions of spermatozoa deposited in her urogenital tract by the father. Mating in most birds does not involve the insertion of a male organ into the female, but rather a simple contact between the two cloacal openings, during which the male's seminal fluids are passed from one body into the other. The sperm cells swim or are drawn up into the oviduct, where actual fertilization occurs. Then in rapid succession great reorganizations take place within the fertilized ovum, including the all-important intermingling of parental chromosomes; and the two-in-one cell begins to divide.

As the tiny bundle of cells, riding on the surface of the yolk, starts passing down the coiled oviduct, albumin is piled around it by special glands in the duct wall, so that the embryo may have nourishment on which to grow during its days of shell confinement. The egg is laid, and incubation is begun. Blood vessels connected to the embryo, and comparable to those in the mammalian placenta, grow out in a network over the surface of the yolk to absorb its nutritious concentrate. Other capillary beds, clinging closely to the inner surface of the shell, act as temporary lungs, for atmospheric oxygen readily diffuses inward through the porous shell and there comes into direct contact with the blood, and expired gases go in the reverse direction; thus the embryo breathes.

Within about 21 days, when the original fertilized germ has produced a cell progeny totaling billions, all properly differentiated and organized into tissues and organs, the eggshell will crack and the young bird will emerge to meet its parents and eventually the hostile world.

My preoccupation the day before had been with violence and death. Today, only a step away in both Freudian and biological sequence, it was with reproduction. Everything around me—the nests, the eggs, the brooders, the seeking males, the willing females, the two mating birds I had watched from a distance as our canoe had approached the garcero that morning—everything here was sex or sex-impelled. Surely nothing new in this, I was well aware. If my blind had been set up in Times Square, I could have made almost precisely the same observation.

But it was not the so-called ugly-headed details of the sex matter that were uppermost in my thoughts. Rather, I fell to musing on the over-all biological significance of sex, be it in bird, man or tulip. Those 10,000 red flying things out there vibrantly reflected the lust to propagate; unconsciously they operated on the knowledge that there was but "little while to stay." In this, their brief moment, they were in one sense cheating death; for while they themselves would within a few years die and pass out of the earthly picture, the species would go on. That was the impelling thing.

But what, in a broader sense, is the meaning of reproduction? Why did nature grant her higher creatures little more time than to reproduce before turning them back into dust? Why is the vital energy of life focused on the perpetuation not of self but of race? And why did nature impose a rigid bisexual system on most animals, when, as is well known, there are other equally effective ways in which organisms may reproduce?

Omitting consideration of viruses and the bacteria (which also at times exhibit sexual characteristics), the first evolutionary step toward the type of sexuality we know so familiarly in vertebrates almost certainly involved the development in some ancient one-celled form of a nucleus in which the heredity-bearing materials—that is, the genes —were concentrated—an event that is thought to have occurred between one and two billion years ago. Primitive or archaic organisms of this sort surviving today are typified by *Chlamydomonas,* a unicellular green alga, and *Crypto-monas,* a single-celled relative of the brown algae.

The behavior of these and other somewhat more complex living species permits us to speculate that, as the next step up the ladder of sexual evolution, a cell floating somewhere in still warm seas or secreted in some moist rock niche was converted into one or more spermlike forms capable of swimming by means of whipping tails. Once liberated, such a swimmer may have set out to explore the waters surrounding the colony in which its parent cell had arisen. What impelled so venturesome a trip is not known, but there is sufficient evidence to infer that the swimmer finally, with delicate tendrils disintegrating, settled on a ledge or, perhaps, a sand grain somewhere along its path and proceeded by simple division to multiply until a new colony like the parent one had been formed. No new genetic material was added or subtracted during this reproductive process; but it was a presex innovation in that the principle of sperm motility was employed, a decisive principle because it enabled the species to spread over wider areas and into more favorable environments than had previously been possible.

The beginning of literal sex came when, presumably as the result of another series of genetic changes, something happened in one of the swimming microbes and it was powerfully attracted to another produced by an alien colony. These two came together and fused—and the way to higher sexuality was firmly established. The now two-in-one organism divided into other individuals which, after swimming about for a time, settled down to form new colonies.

There were no structural differences among those earliest courting cells; they differed only in invisible chemical ways. But obvious external differences, as the final step in the emergence of sex as we know it, were eventually to arise (evidenced today in algae of the *Oedogonium* type). Certain sex cells became larger and less motile than others —and the reality of femaleness and maleness was truly at hand. Also a process called maturation developed somewhere along the way which allowed each marriageable cell only half of the species' characteristic number of chromosomes. Sexual union of a male and a female cell not only re-established the species' full chromosome number, but, more important, accomplished the mingling of genes from two different lines. Throughout subsequent evolution, animals and most plants came to produce large, relatively immobile, nutrient-filled female cells localized in specific organs, while small, often motile male cells were similarly housed until ready for release.

These fundamental male and female innovations laid down a general pattern which resulted in the adoption of bisexuality among higher organisms as their sole method of reproduction.

Why the two-sex system prevailed appears to hinge on the efficiency with which it provided for adaptive variety among living things. To illustrate, suppose that the higher animals were sexless, with reproduction in all individuals of any species consisting of nothing more than the passage into an incubating uterus of a germinal cell now and then, there to undergo a fatherless embryonic growth until birth. That this Huxleyan fancy is in no violation of physiological feasibility is evidenced by experimentation in which ova of rabbits, frogs and other animals have been fertilized artificially by chemical means and have produced offspring without the intermediation of sperm or male stimulus of any kind. With a reproductive system of this kind, each offspring, except in rare cases, has been the exact duplicate of its parent, for no new genetic material was introduced during the process. Such genetic inflexibility obviously would have stifled evolution to the point where it could not possibly have occurred on a vast scale.

The nature of the forces that cause genes to change, so permitting species to adapt or evolve, is not wholly understood. Most prominent today among the various explanations to account for evolutionary change is the concept of mutations. A mutation does not spring from the mere mingling of chromosomes, but from specific changes in the chemical structure of hereditary molecules, changes transmitted thereafter from generation to succeeding generation. Mutations are known to be produced by a variety of ambient physical and chemical forces. High-energy radiations from radioactive elements and cosmic rays which from the beginning of time have been bombarding the cells and tissues of the earth's inhabitants are capable of smashing into dividing chromosomes and causing molecular disruptions that result in changes of a permanent nature. Certain chemicals also may produce such effects, and high temperature may increase the mutation rate. In addition, fragmentation of chromosomal particles during sexual maturation, and the arrangement of their relative positions within the nucleus, may give rise to what seem to be new hereditary characters.

Normally, of course, no offspring can possess characteristics not genetically latent in its parents—just as no matter how many times one throws a conventional pair of dice, only numbers of from two to twelve can come up. But mutations may etch new numbers on the dice. Mutations appear to be entirely random and undirected; for every advantageous mutation there must have been innumerable disadvantageous ones that often led to the extinction of their bearers.

As to the rate of evolution, paleontology is full of instances where evolution seems to have been rapid, other instances where it has been slow or even static. Whatever the factors controlling the rate of evolution, there is little doubt that the system of male-female reproduction, in making possible an intermingling of mutations and variations in one family line with those of another, permits a far wider range of differing individuals within a given species than would be possible if the species were limited to nonsexual reproduction. Throughout the history of life on this planet, wide variation within sexually produced and mutating populations has allowed the greatest advantage in the struggle for existence and has thus rendered species capable of changing and of radiating into the earth's manifold and constantly shifting environments. The biological phenomenon of sex provides not only a means of reproduction, but also the keystone for the process of organic evolution.

Striking me as thematic to the garcero and its ferment of reproducing scarlet birds was the transience of living things. Every one of these scarlet individuals would within a very few years be dead and gone, its pigments returned to the ashes and dust from which they had arisen. How like the beauty of a sunset! The species *G. rubra* might within a few thousand years evolve into something quite different from the lovely colored bird abundant here, might even become extinct. I thought of mankind on whom the forces of organic evolution and transience also play—man who, like all sexually reproducing organisms, evolved by means of variation, mutation and selection but whose present status compares radically with that of any of his animal predecessors or collaterals.

When man emerged from primate and subhuman existence to become a subjective and self-aware animal, the play of organic evolution on his destiny was certainly thereby altered. Endowed now with unique intellectual powers and apparent free will, he found himself capable, at least to some extent, of rejecting the old jungle values of competitive survival and competitive reproduction. One might speculate that under the generalized but by no means wholly applied ethic of "love thy neighbor" man has tended to shift or perhaps even to vitiate his organic destiny. From generation to generation the human species still continues to exhibit a wide spectrum of genetic variations, to produce a heterogeneity of individuals; but in the absence of a means for effective natural selection, one is at a loss to see how further organic change can occur, at least to the extent of producing any new species under the genus *Homo*. The possibility exists that mankind will someday embark on a program of euthenic or selective breeding. Such a course could give rise to a neoevolution whose goals, man-conceived, would surely worry the gods.

But as I looked out over this bird world the matter of the remote evolutionary destiny of either man or the scarlet ibis was, again, far outweighed by that of the individual's transience. Easily explained is the unimportance in nature of the single organism—that is, the precedence, the right of

way, of the species. Is the human individual, like all biological creatures, a perennially expendable entity, with no
significance beyond that which the single organism has
always had as the pawn of evolution? As a biologist, I
had no basis for any other than an affirmative answer. As
all too human a being, I found such an answer violently
unsatisfactory.

There is a man of my acquaintance (a paleontologist)
who once remarked in my presence that whenever he al-
lows his mind's eye to probe backward into the stagger-
ingly vast history of organic evolution on this planet, the
illusion of his own individual importance melts away.
Philosophically, he considers himself to be not much more
than a 170-pound lump of integrated protoplasm produced
during some two billion years of interplay between environmental change and organic adaptation; a vertebrate whose
capacity for thought and introspection, although no doubt
exceeding that of his nonhomoid collaterals or antecedents,
is far too limited to grasp even remotely the meaning of
life; a gene carrier in a trillion-runner relay with the finish-
ing tape nowhere in sight; a mammal perhaps a bit too pre-
cocious for his own good.

A diametrically opposed point of view is taken by those
who subscribe to fundamentalist religion, who hold high
all the tested human virtues, believing that philosophical
dilemmas can be resolved only on the basis of religious
faith. Good and evil are absolute values defined by the
conscience; organic evolution is a method God employed
for the primary purpose of creating soul-endowed human
beings, each of whom will someday be judged according to
his conduct here on earth.

On the other hand, there are others who bow only to

knowledge intellectually derived, who believe that mankind's only hope lies in the continuing quest for rational
truth as revealed by the methods of objective science. With
such issues as ultimate truth, purpose, religion and so on
we are not yet ready to cope. Only when we know virtually
all there is to know about the physical universe (a goal
that some believe is actually attainable) will the nature of
man's so-called spirituality be revealed.

Still others argue that both the conventionally religious
and the intellectual approaches to phenomena are themselves delusory; only the mystical has meaning. Truth may
be perceived but fractionally by the intellect; hence it is
unknowable on a mental plane. A conception of truth, in its
infinitude, may be realized only within the fabric of meta-
physics.

That men are able to contemplate so variously the meaning of life, are able to rationalize the individual's transience, able to recognize that time exists on both sides of
the present—these are perhaps in themselves evidences
that the human individual is more than the mere victim of
evolution's disregard. That man suspects the existence of
factors in the universe that are far beyond his capacity
to understand is classically cited as an indication that they
do in fact exist.

My first serious photographic efforts finally got under way
on my fourth day in the garcero. The tripod was crowded
alongside me on the hidden table. Such other necessary
adjuncts to bird photography as long focal-length lenses,
filters, film cartridges, a light meter, etc., bulged my jacket
pockets. There were no shelves in this studio; camera case
and all other of my immediate worldly possessions were in

the canoe, now secluded from sight in some distant corner of the swamp.

Finally after a couple of near spills I was ready to proceed. Focusing the eight-inch telephoto lens on a handsome bird drowsing on her nest ten or twelve feet away, I prayed for an interval of sunlight. Although the sky was full of clouds, they were not static, and here and there were gaps of blue. Finally the sun broke through one of these, and the garcero was full of glory. Exposure calculations were quickly made, diaphragm was adjusted, shutter speed was set—and I began to shoot. Photographically good sun is rare in these parts, so I worked fast. First there was the brooder, then the more distant flying groups, then the bushes with the young on top, then the standers, the arrivers, the leavers, the nests, the eggs—every aspect of bird life that came within range of my ground glass.

For almost a full hour the sun favored me, which was something of a break. But then, inevitably, the sky filled again, and camera efforts came to an abrupt halt. As though in anticipation of bad weather, my model of the moment buried her beak and head deep under one wing. Manuel and Ventura had orders that on the threat of general rain they were to return and pick me up. But through none of the various peepholes could I see any sign of the canoe; they no doubt construed the overcast as temporary and the impending rain as local.

There was nothing I could do but wait, either for the canoe or for a clearing sky. I squirmed a bit to relieve tired muscles, careful not to tip the tripod or the table. I had just finished putting the cap on the lens and a cover over the camera when the rain began. My bird, gone from the ground glass but still to be seen directly through the peephole, faded into the cascade. The umbrella fulfilled its secondary purpose to perfection and, although I felt like one sitting under Niagara, I remained dry. Brushing off mosquitoes had long since become second nature to me. Now, for a while, I became aware of these pests again, along with the heat and the heavy, sweaty humidity.

For the first time in the course of my llanos trials I recognized the symptoms of slight nostalgia, not only for the comforts of home but for the work I had left behind. I thought almost tenderly of my white mice in their clean laboratory cages, of my strains of transplantable tumors, of my efforts, along with those of many another research man these days, to make sense out of the mystery of cancerous growth. It occurred to me, in regard to the very ibis embryos I had examined a day or two before, that if it were known precisely under what influences the cells in those embryos were developing—how, say, some became muscle tissue, others, skin tissue; what in the normal ibis body prevents cells from undergoing unauthorized growth—perhaps a solution to the cancer enigma would be at hand. Tissue specialization within the embryo, the play of chemical organizers in determining the direction and extent of development during growth—these, whether referring to *Guara rubra* or *Homo sapiens*, are close to the heart of the whole cancer matter. Plants may develop cancer, as may fish, amphibians, birds and mammals—right across the board. Wherever there is tissue growth there is the possibility of cancer. It is a fundamental manifestation, and one certainly not limited to the tissues of man. Accordingly, the problem of abnormal growth has ceased being the exclusively medical one of years past, and today is as much the concern of the experimental biologist as it is of the practicing physician.

Much of what was previously called cancer research was a quest for means by which to destroy or to limit the growth of anarchistic tissues. Successful therapy must be destructive to malignant cells without at the same time being harmful to normal tissues. Attempts at therapy have been made since the days of Hippocrates. Medical literature, both ancient and modern, is virtually glutted with "cures," none of which has stood up under test. Today only a few partially effective clinical measures are recognized. Of these, surgery is the oldest, the crudest but perhaps still the most useful. X rays, neutrons and the like get into deep tissues beyond reach of the knife, and various radioactive materials may be applied even closer to the site of the trouble; but the ever-present hazard in the use of these potent energies lies in the possibility of damaging normal tissues. The search for better killing agents goes on and is supremely justified from the viewpoint of healing. Yet fundamental research is not concerned so much with "what to do about cancer" as with "why does it occur?"

The modern laboratory approach to this "why?" involves one or all of several basic hypotheses. The first holds that, preceding cancer, something changes within the culpable cells, rendering them indifferent to the internal regulating agencies that keep the cells and tissues of the healthy body under tight physiological control. If such a change were genetic, all the descendants of any cell so altered would bear the fatal mark. In this connection, a great amount of experimental work has been done on the problem of heredity and cancer. As yet no sweeping generalizations may be drawn. There are many pure-bred strains of mice, rats, fish, etc., in which cancer develops generation after generation in strict conformity to known laws of heredity. Susceptibility to growth aberrancy in the tissues involved is obviously passed from parent to offspring. On the other hand, there are strains of mice, rats and fish inherently immune to cancer. The nature of the mechanism behind this susceptibility in one strain, and the resistance in another, continues to be one of the most pressing as well as most baffling problems of genetics.

A second broad working hypothesis under test by the laboratory experimentalist suggests that something has changed within the control systems of the body. It is known, for example, that cells of breast tissue are subject to at least partial control of hormones passed into the blood stream by the pituitary and ovarian glands. If the chemical temperaments of these hormones change, so will the control that they exert over breast tissues. A corresponding, but in most cases still obscurely understood, regulatory system must exist for every tissue type in the body; and defects in such systems may similarly permit cells under their jurisdiction to revert to laxity—and cancer.

A third operating hypothesis holds that an irritating agent enters the body or is possibly released by some subtly malfunctioning tissue. For example, many chemicals are known which, when applied to the skin, will mysteriously cause the cells with which they come into contact to react malignantly. A classic example is the case of chimney sweeps in eighteenth-century England who, because of certain hydrocarbons in the soot with which their skin came into daily contact, developed a high incidence of skin cancer.

A fourth hypothesis is an extension of the third, the irritating agent here considered to be of so complex a nature as actually to resemble a living virus. Such "viruses," when and where they exist, are fragile and unstable and, with few exceptions, have defied isolation or even detection. Of the four known today, one produces cancer in chickens, one in rabbits and one in frogs—curiously, in a different organ of each species. The fourth, and perhaps the most impressive, is found in certain strains of laboratory mice, and is transmitted from generation to generation through the mother's milk. This factor causes no immediate sickness upon entering the body; in fact, its presence can scarcely be divined by known laboratory methods. The real evidence for its lethal action is that mice getting the infected milk invariably develop mammary cancer during the second half of their lives, and die. If, instead, they are suckled by foster mothers of a cancer-free strain, no cancer develops.

It would be falsely optimistic to state that there is any immediate hope for a general explanation of, or an over-all cure for, cancer—mainly because there are so many varieties of the manifestation. To discover, for example, that a virus causes breast cancer in the mouse is no reason for supposing that a virus exists for, say, bone cancer. Possibly the latter type of cancer will be found to result from some sort of physiological malfunctioning. Or because mouse breast cancer is transmitted by a virus is no reason for assuming that a transmitted virus is involved in human breast cancer. Each type of malignancy probably has its own cause, or complex of causes, and is likely to have its own explanation and treatment.

Portrait of a
Scarlet Ibis.

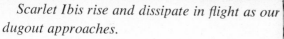

Scarlet Ibis rise and dissipate in flight as our dugout approaches.

A parent arrives to feed its nearly grown still bush-bound young.

This young ibis has not yet learned to fly. There is no hint of the superb coloration of adulthood

The author and his outboard and a scarlet captive.

Camera with self-timer catches author's daily entrance to the birdblind.

At each synchronized lunge, run, and push of the pole, the 20-foot long dugout yielded with a powerful spurt ahead.

While showering dignity and color on the Scarlet Ibis, nature seems to have been reluctant in the bestowal of weapons. The bird's beak is blunt, its toenails

unsharpened, and its eyes have a gentle, soft, bambi quality. The White Ibis at extreme left is considered to be a separate species, since it does not interbreed with its scarlet counterpart.

Recalling the words of others privileged to have been among Scarlet Ibis, I felt that the beauty of these birds was not solely a function of my own susceptibilities.

Wingtips and nest clutch of the Scarlet Ibis.

© *National Geographic Magazine*

Three queer birds of the deep llanos: the hoatzin (above), the boat-billed night heron (below), and (right) a maguari stork upon its nesting mound.

Cancer is an unhappy subject. But as I sat in the blind that afternoon, having, because of bad weather, allowed my thoughts to wander, it was evident to me that, although the body of man was created in the chemical and biological image of his evolutionary forebears and so is subject to their ancient frailties, there is a special dimension in human make-up that seeks always to dispel darkness, physical or philosophical. Cancer and other sore afflictions to which flesh is heir? They cannot fail ultimately to yield; in this I am at one with the disciples of objective science. As to the subjective dilemmas that beset mankind—resolution of these may have to await the second coming.

Chapter 8

BREAKING the garcero's monotony of thornbushes were occasional trees which, because of their smooth white bark
and lobed leaves, I assumed to be some variety of wild fig.
They extended considerably above the average height of
the garcero's other vegetation, and it was for this reason,
several days later, that I found myself perched up near
the top of one of them, from where I commanded a view
not only of the entire garcero but of the surrounding
swampland as well. From here I could see sights previously
denied me: groups of anhingas, glossy ibises and even
maguari storks living in vegetation peripheral to the primary scarlet-ibis community. Above and beyond that, in
the sky, were the familiar undulating lines of scarlet, beginning as dots or becoming dots in the far southeast.
Here and there I could see a great maguari stork rise pon-
derously from its bush and take to the air, probably off
on a food mission. I could see cruel-faced snakebirds—
anhingas—ministering to their nestbound young with the
same gentle care that a doe would give her fawn. I could
see shrubs draped in a somber black covering of glossy ibises
—non-*Guara* cousins of the scarlet and white ibises—whose
nigrescent plumage seemed here to have given the bearers
a segregated status. And in the more immediate neigh-
borhood—ahead, right, left, behind—were the red birds,
loading every bush, sagging every branch. I could feel the

tremor of life as 10,000 entities proceeded to the fulfillment of 10,000 discrete destinies.

The sight had a magnifying effect; and I felt a little like one taken to a very high place and shown the kingdoms of the world. I was not aware of any tempter offering me these kingdoms in return for my soul, but for a fleeting moment I cast aside objectivity and absorbed beauty and vastness as values in a sphere apart; there was an element of something transcendent here. Trite pantheism, I chided myself. Forget it, and get on with the bird watching. But for another second or two I hesitated, feeling as one possessed of two levels of awareness. I do not know why the sight of birds, however many and impressive, should during that moment of introversion have suffused a shadow into the recesses of my personal philosophy. Perhaps I was tired, depleted. The llanos are known to have that effect. Whatever the physiological or psychological basis for my mood, it was with an effort that I continued, as demanded, with the proper business.

The tree that I chose to call—lacking a botanic field guide—a wild fig was sparsely leafed (no doubt the result of water suffocation) and, accordingly, an excellent observation tower. I had managed, with the aid of some adroit hoisting from Ventura, to get hold of the tree's lower branches, and before long I was some twenty feet into the air, lowering a twine to the men in the canoe below. Up without mishap came first the telephoto camera, then the binoculars. These tools of the trade securely in hand, and my body stabilized crotch to crotch where a large branch forked from the trunk, I settled down for a good look around.

I had seen those maguari storks from a distance several times during our daily travels to and from the garcero, but, being wholly intent on the scarlet birds, I had previously given them only minor consideration. Now, over an area of perhaps a square half mile, I counted no less than fifty single derby-hatlike bushes inhabited by what, in comparison with the ibises all around, seemed like a race of avian giants. Specific examination through the glasses confirmed this impression.

Each derby, some six feet high and eight feet across, had its top squashed in by a heavy nest of whorled fagots. Adding decoration to some of the hats were garlands of pale-blue morning-glory blossoms. These storks, while not so large as the soldier species I had seen elsewhere in the llanos, were nevertheless behemoths in comparison with the numerically predominating *Guara* birds. Where a stork was in a brooding position, the presence of eggs was indicated; but where the adult was standing, I could invariably see young: one or two lumps of jet-black feathers or down. These were conspicuous through the glasses, for (as with nestlings of all bird species) the preoccupation of baby storks is aggressively with the larder. I could see the clumsy bodies of ebony velvet rising and lowering in the nest, scissor beaks agape and stretched high in a gesture that could not be misconstrued.

Each giant standing alert and protective above its begging progeny had at least one qualification for presuming to reside in the vicinity of the scarlet ibis. An area of naked scarlet skin surrounded each glinting yellow iris. This, together with a similarly colored skin patch under the chin, gave to each stork the facial aspect of some sort of harlequined devil. The remainder of the plumage was snowy on the upper parts of the body, coal black on the lower back and outer wing halves.

While these small but vivid touches of scarlet tied the storks into the general color scheme of the ibis settlement, other features were in striking contrast—among these not only beak shape, leg form and body manner, but also flight movement. No churning of wings as one of these beak-weaponed creatures took off; rather, a slow involution of pinions, which reminded me of a Dutch windmill turning under a slow but certain wind.

My binoculars scanned across this suburb of giants, then into the swarming city of littler red birds, then, like a panning movie lens, down into the garcero where the water was patched with floating plants and green algal scum. I became aware, as rarely before, of the enormous size difference between these several and extreme forms of living things in my environment. I compared the storks, among the largest of flying birds, and the algae, about the smallest life visible from my tree perch; then I took a step farther into a comparison of other even bigger and even smaller creatures. What of the whale weighing many tons, or the sequoia reaching up over two hundred feet into the sky? And at the other end of the size range, what of the tiniest bacterium, barely visible through the compound microscope and weighing only billionths of a gram?

On initial consideration, from bacterium to whale seemed like an enormous size range for nature to have chosen in which to animate her subjects; but further reflection suggested that it was in fact an exceedingly narrow one. The bacterium is still trillions of times bigger than one of the atoms comprising it; the whale is a mere dot on the sea, the sequoia but a splinter on the side of a mountain.

In addition to filling the dimension range so familiar to us, why did not organisms evolve to sizes even smaller than the bacterium and even larger than the whale?

Such questions are certainly not original with me. I suspect that they have occurred and reoccurred ever since man first started brooding over the mysterious world of which he is so unimpressively small an inhabitant. Swift's fantasia into the realm of the Lilliputians and the Brobdingnagians, or the medieval scholar's speculations on how many angels can dance on the point of a needle, suggest a deep-seated quandary in the mind of man over the meaning of his organic and structural limitations. Do the universal legends of giants and skyscraping beanstalks perhaps imply an unconscious human reluctance to accept the six-foot, 180-pound blueprint?

One viewpoint in this regard is based on atomic and molecular physics and starts with the well-supported assumption that all matter on this planet, animate and inanimate, is composed of some ninety different varieties of atoms. Where several types of atoms, or elements, have affinity for one another and combine in some orderly pattern, a configuration results which we call a molecule; and heaps of similar cohering molecules become the compounds of everyday familiarity.

But despite the seeming homogeneity that our senses ascribe to such compounds, the comprising atoms, while maintaining their ordinarily fixed positions within each molecule, are nevertheless in a state of continuous thermal agitation. If temperature is raised beyond certain defined limits (different for each variety of molecule), the agitation increases until at length atoms will leap from their molecular positions and the compound will disintegrate. When a piece of bread is held over a flame, carbon atoms break out of starch molecules, for example, to appear as black crust; oxygen, hydrogen and other atoms of the molecules comprising the bread components stream off as gases or recombine to form relatively more simple molecules.

According to modern physics, the quivering of atoms is purely random, and there can be no assumption as to the precise position of any specific atom at any specific instant, and hence no predicting of its reaction to any external force at any given instant. On the other hand, the simultaneous movement of a great many like atoms sets up an average quivering. Thus—if the idea does not suffer too much from so utter a simplification—the larger the number of atoms (and/or molecules) in any particle of matter, the more predictable is the behavior of that particle in respect to external forces; conversely, the smaller the number of atoms, the less predictable. Carried to its extreme, a mass of matter consisting of one separate atom becomes a physically disorderly thing whose movements are indeterminative. The upshot is that an organism made up of, say, only ten atoms—or, better, molecules—could not possibly react to physical and chemical energies with a sufficient degree of exactitude and orderliness to sustain the finely balanced integration required of living matter.

Then suppose our hypothetical organism were made up of a thousand atoms. Such an entity would respond to energy laws with relatively more regularity than the ten-atom entity—as, analogously, the outcome of a thousand coin flips is more accurately predictable than that of ten. An organism comprising 100,000 atoms would be, by the same reasoning, an even more reliable reaction system. But even this number would still fall far short of sustaining the molecular and atomic regularity essential for metabolic processes.

That the smallest bacterium (which by easy calculation can be established as containing in the order of trillions of atoms) approaches the size threshold below which cellular life cannot be sustained is suggested by studies employing the high-speed centrifuge, the electron microscope, extremely fine filters and special culturing techniques—for, although these instruments and methods reveal in nature an untold number of particles smaller than bacteria, no such particles are strictly cells nor do they exhibit the reproductive and metabolic characteristics expected of cellular organisms. These particles (viruses, bacteriophages and such entities as genes—all vastly smaller than the smallest bacterium) must for growth and reproduction always be a functional part of more complex protoplasm; they are incapable of living independently, and can exist only as parasites within true cells. That a gene, containing far fewer atoms than we assume to be necessary for cellular life, can retain its vital structural and functional integrity generation after generation has been explained by the eminent physicist Schrödinger on the basis of its being, actually, an aperiodic crystal—which is where the biologist may appropriately leave the subject to others.

But to add one further thought, it is surely not atomic and molecular statistics alone that set a lower limit on the size of living cells. Consider that most protoplasm for successful operation must contain atoms of some 30 to 40 different elements, and in such combination that carbon or oxygen, for example, may have to be present in ratio to magnesium, say, as ten thousand to one. Consider, in addition, the diversity of molecular structures needed for metabolism—the proteins, carbohydrates, vitamins, minerals, enzymes; the colloids, gels, etc. An independent living system lives because it is capable of deriving energy from its surroundings, energy which it can modify for its own special use. Such a system apparently can so operate only when it has attained a molecular complexity prescribed by the nature and requirements of energy transferences among its variously constituted components. A mechanical calculator can perform specific complex integrations only when a certain minimal number of appropriate vacuum tubes, relays, feedbacks, etc., are provided. So with the living cell.

Now, how about those storks, whales and redwoods? Why are there no whales the size of the *Queen Elizabeth,* no men as tall as windmills? Here the answer is easier. Consider first the food problem to be faced by any behemoth. Single-cell organisms secure nutrient by direct absorption of energy-laden molecules dissolved in the watery fluids in which these creatures live. This classical method of feeding is suitable so long as the dimensions of the feeder stay within certain fixed trigonometric limits— limits defined by the mathematical relation between a sphere's surface and its volume; that is, there is a very specific size maximum beyond which the volume of protoplasm within any sphere exceeds the capacity of its absorbing surface to feed.

Thus when nature chose to increase the size of her earliest creations, she had to do so not by swelling the volume of each single cell, but rather by causing numbers of such cells to cohere. The resulting multicellular organism, with many of its cell surfaces now facing inward away from the nutrient-bearing medium, required new and more complex quartermaster methods which, of course, developed accordingly. The most successful of these among animals appears to have been the one employing the tube-within-a-tube principle. The outer tube comprised what we call the body; the inner tube became a tract through which ingested food passed, the while yielding up its load of nutrient.

But in the course of evolution, as animals thus equipped with straight digestive tubes grew larger, they began to have difficulty absorbing enough food to satisfy the needs of their increased bulk, or they were unable physiologically to deliver nourishment where needed. Thereupon the intestinal tract was lengthened, coiled and creased to provide yet greater area for absorption; in addition, pumps and pipelines for circulating the absorbed nutrient began to develop, so that every tissue and cell surface within the body might be reached.

Such revolutionary changes encouraged, via either cause or effect, the development of stronger supportive skeletons and more powerful muscles. Reciprocally, the greater the over-all body mass, the larger and bulkier the feeding department needed to be. Such seesaw evolution continued, and many animals and plants eventually increased in size until they were comparatively monstrous. Two factors finally served to clamp a lid on size evolution: the first, in animals, was a limited food supply, and the second and more fundamental were the laws of gravity, hydrostatics and mechanics.

Animals of dinosaur pattern, in order to furnish their enormous and clumsy hulks with adequate nourishment, had not only to feed almost continuously, but for support had to rest their bellies on bog and swamp muds. It is an everyday fact that while a toothpick is stiff and relatively inflexible, a sliver of wood of the same thickness as a toothpick but ten feet in length is quite flexible and will break of its own weight if lifted in the middle. It is this character of gravity and mass that prevented the vertebrate backbone from evolving to greater lengths than it did. A backbone a hundred feet long would require for support and movement so enormous a muscular system as to have been unnourishable. Snakes long ago gave up trying to lift a long backbone; and whales depend on water buoyancy for help. Among land animals, the elephant, giraffe and rhino represent the approximate maximum weight and size sustainable.

Consider the even greater problems of an erect giant. The 60-foot Brobdingnagians of Swift's fancy were conceived in Gulliver's same human proportions. It is calculable that a 60-foot human colossus would weigh some 90 tons, a weight in no way supportable by humanly proportioned bones even if fashioned of iron and actuated by muscles of steel. With his first step such a "man" would have crashed to the earth of his own mass. In order for a 60-foot man to stand erect and walk, his construction would have to resemble that of a microcephalic creature afflicted monstrously with elephantiasis—his head tiny, neck short, shoulders narrow, pelvis enormously broad and thick, legs and feet positively mountainous. At best, such a living pyramid could move only at a lumbering gait. The mouth—even with continuous feeding—could not possibly devour enough to keep the system going. And need we mention the difficulties such a creature would encounter in matters of blood circulation, excretion, vision, hearing, etc.?

Among birds the principles of aerodynamics, not to think of the mechanics of feather construction, would have beaten back any adventurers into gianthood. Flamingos, storks and swans are about at the top of the size heap.

More ambitious birds have invariably lost their flight powers, as witness the ostriches and the extinct moas of New Zealand.

As to size limits in the world of plants, the largest living vertical species are the California sequoia and the Australian bald cypress. Horizontal forms, like the mangrove, may have total bulks exceeding these, and some of the creepers extend over vast areas. But here, as in animal forms, the limitations of food supply plus the rulings of physics and chemistry pretty well obviate the possibility of giant beanstalks.

One is pressed to the conclusion that, since life's origin, organisms have exploited nearly every potential of gravity, surface tension, hydrostatics, mechanics, etc.—emerging after two billion years as an incredibly variegated spectrum of species, but squeezed into what actually amounts to an exceedingly narrow range of dimension and volume.

My treetop considerations that afternoon did not extend to include size limits on angels. I felt reasonably sure that matters of food supply and physics in heaven bear little comparison with those here on earth.

One morning a brainstorm impelled me to untie and recommission my little flat-bottomed boat which since the trip from Matapalos had lain unused on the riverbank in front of Manuel's hut. I proposed to tow it to the garcero and there to rig it with the umbrella and monk's cloth. So equipped, it would serve as a sort of houseboat-blind, floatable to whatever bush in the bird swamp I wished to observe. But the effort ended ingloriously with the prospective blind support getting stuck in the first tangle of jungle roots we encountered. After a good deal of pushing, pulling, poling and punting, we extricated the craft, floated her downriver and deposited her back up on the Algarrobito mudbank. The attempt educated me as to why, for llanos swamp travel, dugouts are preferred over wide-beam craft. One's boat must not only be capable of doing to underbrush what a needle does to cloth, but it must be heavy enough to have the inertia properties of a battering ram.

This floating-blind notion may have reflected a growing resistance on my part to being perched for hours and days on a half-submerged platform of dubious stability. True, I did not see a single caribe during my whole garcero sojourn, but the constant awareness of their presence was not stimulating to my peace of mind. On more than one occasion a sudden off-center body movement almost tipped both platform and bird watcher into the forbidden waters. I think it was the evening after one of those incidents that the floating-blind idea occurred to me, an idea whose abandonment seemed as brilliant as had its synthesis.

Our route to and from the garcero, via proper dugout, was not the same on any two voyages. In principle, we would set out up the Matillure, succeeding against the current by use of the outboard. This remarkable converter of chemical energy into mechanical thrust was screwclamped to the dugout's fungus-weakened end plate. On our very first trip I had connected a safety line between the motor chassis and a solid brace board amidships. But, happily, my fear that a portion of the rotting stern might give way, allowing the motor tragically and prematurely to find final rest in the Matillure's muddy bottom, proved in the end to be without justification.

Each day before sunrise we would proceed upriver to

where, about a half mile distant from Algarrobito, we
would come to a certain vaguely recognizable thinning
of the north-bank foliage. I would steer directly for this,
giving the craft at that moment full benefit of a wide-open
throttle. Then off with the ignition, up with the prop and
down with all heads. Except for the dull scrapings of wet
wood against wet wood as the canoe bludgeoned its way
into the tangle, a silence would quickly set in as though
some sort of sound-absorbing curtain had suddenly fallen.
Then all movement would stop, which was a cue for the
men to get up and work. Muscle power now took over
as they seized branches, roots, trunks, anything within
reach alongside the boat, and pulled us into a dusky world
of naked arches, face-slapping leaves and trailing lianas.
Our course and progress here were wholly opportunistic.
But sooner or later we would intercept some little half-
open artery and the men would use their poles or, if the
water were too deep, their paddles. At last, having penetrated the Matillure's belt of bank jungle, we would break
out into open grass country.

To speak of this grass country as open is a gross inaccu-
racy, for nothing is less open than llanos flood plains toward
the end of the wet season when the great *Paspalum* grasses
have reached their seasonal maximum. Spearing six to
eight feet above water, millions—billions—of narrow shafts
create a vast viridian forest, penetrable only via little drainage channels that twist and turn through the grass.

On my first intimate grapple with the high-grass swamp
I felt like one in the midst of Bunyan's Slough of Despond.
No guide marks of any sort were visible from canoe level,
and there was no way of seeing up and over. The venule

we had been following had come to a narrowing dead end.
Which way to turn now? The men put down their paddles,
embarrassed and self-conscious over the error; they had
been traveling by dead reckoning or on the basis of a dry-
season knowledge of the terrain and district. At length
Ventura stood up to full height, straddling the canoe gunwales, then slowly turned his head, with eyes fixed on the
far sky at as low an angle as the grass tops would permit.
Within five seconds he was pointing emphatically to the
right, and within another ten our canoe bow was spearing
into the grass there. Before the canoe's stern end was out
of the original venule its fore end was already breaking
into the open of a larger channel, immediately recognized
by all of us as our regular highway, the one leading past
a familiar knoll, and ultimately to the less choked waters
around the garcero. The cue Ventura had searched for and
found had been the garcero-Algarrobito bird line. Once we
had determined our position in relation to it, orientation
had been simple. The fact that we had unknowingly been
separated from the main channel by a vegetation barrier
less thick than the length of the canoe is an indication of
the grass's density.

Such travel routine as this, repeated twice daily, plus the
long vigils of watching, photographing and ruminating in
the blind, led me before long to think of taking a little time
off. And, too, the weather had been brutal. Day after day
clouds of gray and black continued to roll low. The number of times I was soaked while en route to or from the
garcero; or the number of times the image of a bird in the
ground glass or the peephole changed from clear to misty,
to watery, to gone; or the number of nights I lay in my

Algarrobito hammock listening to a downpour being softened to sad llanos music on the thatched roof—these are now beyond memory.

So came the day that we dismantled the blind, pulled the table from out of the mud and returned all to camp. That evening I took a bath along the river's edge and shaved. My plan was to lie around camp for a few days—perhaps to probe the mud meadows to the southeast in the direction of the presumptive feeding grounds; also to sew up some seams that had rotted open in the monk's cloth. Manuel and Ventura seemed unhappy during the blind demolition, thinking, I suppose, that my visit was coming to an end. I tried to indicate that this was not so, that we would return for more work later in the week.

Urschleim, a word used by nineteenth-century European evolutionists, has always appealed to me. I like its onomatopoësis, but mostly what it means—primordial ooze, a hypothetical stuff that appeared two or so billion years ago as the precursor to protoplasm and life on this planet.

A relationship between the subject of ooze and llanos life presented itself during the first day of my time off from the garcero. By habit, I rolled out of the sleeping net at dawn, slipped on my sandals, ate a breakfast of Chloroquin, canned fruit, biscuits and coffee, and then was ready for activity. My plan for the day had been to clean spark plugs and, in the rain-free comfort of the hut, leisurely to bring my notebook up to date. But the sky was so exquisitely clear (naturally, since no photography was scheduled!) that I decided this was the day to investigate those feeding grounds. Before setting out, I spread the considerably mildewed monk's cloth on the ground outside the hut for

a thorough airing and drying in the promised sun. I re-
quested Manuel to keep an eye on the cloth and, if rain
did come, to take it in. Then I strapped on my canteen belt
and was off.

The eastern sky was at that moment a hemisphere of
light-radiating saffron; overhead were lines of ibises pointing like flights of undeviating arrows to the southeast. What
better signpost than this for guiding one through unfamiliar
terrain? The flat southern horizon toward which I had set
out was broken only by clusters of chaparral here and there
or by small groups of cattle grazing disconsolately on
already well-thinned-out grass. Gone were the tall swamp
grasses, the tangles of marsh jungle, the pervading flood.
This *tierra alta* south of the Matillure was ranch land whose
dominant character this time of year was squashy mud that
oozed up over and into one's sandals. It had a warm, soft,
tickling quality that gave me a peculiar feeling of sensual
comfort, and thereby a momentary insight to the swine's
point of view regarding mire. What brought me to the subject of *Urschleim* was the realization that this ooze lapping
up over my ankles and gushing between my toes was, like
the primordial ooze of two billennia ago, animate. I could
not see them and I could not feel them, but I knew that
with each step I was disrupting the lives of millions of
evolution's latter-day protozoa, bacteria, bacteriophages,
worms, insect larvae, crustacea, etc.

During past weeks my eyes had been on certain of evolution's more advanced inhabitants of this llanos world, my
thoughts often on their characteristics of death, struggle,
size, sex, growth. I was aware now of the life in the mud
wheezing between my toes, and thoughts turned to the
question of how the great tree of organic evolution first

started growing on this planet. As to the origin of my own species, I recalled the unminced words of the vice-chancellor of Cambridge University in 1654: ". . . man was created by the Trinity on the 26th of October, 4004 B.C., at 9 o'clock in the morning."

For a foolish second I wished I had lived in the day of that belief. What a supreme comfort it must have been to know so simply and satisfactorily who and what were responsible for one's being! Creation of man in one swift stroke! Such a God is worthy of worship and awe. In contrast, think of the modern conception of a depersonalized force at work sculpturing life with the tools of violence, reproduction and death! Little wonder that we do not have the kind of respect for the God idea today that we did in the days of fundamentalist theology.

I trudged on through the llanos *Urschleim*, keeping one eye open for feeding birds and the other sadly inverted on thoughts of life's origin. Was it puerile to be saddened by the realization that God is no longer a part of the creation picture; that a bloodless concept of evolution and energy exchange had come to replace Him; that today when a man dies we read no-longer-believed poetry over his remains instead, as in yesteryear, of rejoicing over his ascendency to a literal heaven?

Cosmogonists—inferring, to be sure, but inferring on the basis of some fairly impressive evidence—tell us, among other theories, that some 20 billion years ago this planet was an incandescent fragment of nuclear energy, derived from the sun, which ten billion years later congealed into a hot ball comprising the basic elements. With the passing of about eight billion years more this celestial body descended the thermal scale to the point where metals and rocks hardened and the crust and enveloping atmosphere grew cool. But not until the cooling had progressed down to the temperature at which water could exist in liquid form was the stage set for the development of life.

It is no caprice that life did not appear before then, for protoplasm as we know it can exist only in a milieu of liquid water. On the other hand, there is no basis for either averring or denying that some sort of nonaqueous "life" exists on other celestial bodies. We know only that our kind of life—the kind exhibited by bacterium, scarlet ibis and man—depends for its existence on certain properties of solvency, heat retention, diffusion, surface tension, etc., possessed only by water.

Water is liquid between 0 and 100 degrees C.; hence these limits define the thermal range above and below which protoplasmic life cannot function. In boiling water protoplasm dies, in frozen water it becomes metabolically inert. Most living things do best somewhere between 20 and 38 degrees C., although there are species—such as the algae of steaming sulphur springs and the creatures of the cold oceanic depths—that thrive in one thermal extreme or the other. Organisms such as mammals and birds have internal thermostats which keep their body tissues at a relatively constant temperature regardless of fluctuations on the outside. Most aquatic forms, on the other hand, having no thermostats, adopt the temperature of their surroundings.

When the poet Goethe, plagiarizing the Greeks, wrote that *"Alles ist aus dem Wasser entsprungen"* he was anticipating modern ideas of biogenesis; but he did not (nor as a poet would he have been expected to) provide information as to why water was selected as life's womb. Today we approach this matter in terms of the planet's chemical evolution. When the fiery cloud cooled—one theory holds —a central core developed consisting of heavy elements of the iron and nickel variety. Next, that most remarkable of all the elements, carbon, precipitated out of the earth's white gaseous envelope and, like its heavier predecessors, gravitated toward the center of the planetary mass. Literal blizzards of black dust must have fallen, if this thesis is correct; and as the carbon drifts approached the red-hot core, they came into contact with the heavier metal atoms already there. Immediately the unique combining proclivities of carbon caused it to react with the other elements present to form simple carbide compounds.

The earth's atmosphere at that time was not one of free nitrogen and oxygen, as it is today, but one of superheated steam vapor. The core is considered to have been a shapeless wad of soft lavalike material. However, on further cooling, the surface of this fudge began to harden into a crust which, under the influence of tidal forces exerted by moon and sun, cracked periodically. Great bleeding streams of fiery carbide and metal pressed up through the cracks, spilling over the face of the nascent planet. Here the hot carbides came into contact with the planet's atmosphere, and the reaction between the atmosphere's water vapor and the carbides most certainly gave rise to hydrocarbons, then to alcohols, aldehydes, ketones, organic acids and a host of other compounds implicated in later biochemical processes. As to the origin of the atmosphere's free oxygen, there is no unanimity of opinion.

Some biochemists believe that certain of the newly formed hydrocarbons, together with ammonia, water and hydrogen, interacted to produce at least traces of those all-essential building blocks of protein, the amino acids. This view has received considerable support recently from an experimental demonstration that, when these four compounds are mixed in a closed glass vessel and subjected to high electrical energy, elementary amino acids are indeed produced.

As the temperature of the planet's surface slid below the critical 100° mark, water molecules condensed out of the gaseous state and great mist clouds stormed the face of the earth. Rain fell, depressions filled, seas arose. Immediately dissolving in the earth's new liquid were those previously formed nitrogenous compounds.

But none of these, nor any combination of them, were yet close to constituting living matter. Before even the most rudimentary self-reproducing and growing life entity appeared, there must have been a long period of further synthesis, characterized by the production of proteins out of amino acids and then, as postulated by the biochemist Oparin, by a coming together of protein molecules into tiny aggregates called colloidal particles. From these developed the gels, which in turn came to form the basic texture of later protoplasm. The ultra-small particles or globules comprising these gels were not alive, but they must have had some obscure capacity to "grow" by chemically attracting certain molecules found in the surrounding medium, as do indeed many crystals; certain nonliving membranes show a capacity selectively to absorb dissolved materials and will even undergo a sort of repair to injury.

It is surmised (and from here on the question of life's origin becomes a truly speculative game, for the process has never been observed and indeed may have occurred only once) that the primordial colloid globules "grew" by some such process of absorption and then, in reaction to sphere-volume laws, split into two, somewhat as true living cells do during division. Such "growing" and "reproducing" gelatinous "cells" had yet a long way to go before they could be called living. The usual definition of living matter involves such terms as irritability, metabolism, growth, reproduction, specific internal organization and modifiability.

The last-mentioned property is perhaps the most essential of all from the evolutionary point of view, for, if the preliving gels had not possessed a susceptibility to change, they would, obviously, have developed no further. It is at this point that biogenetic speculation has traditionally run afoul with philosophy. Nineteenth-century thinkers of strong vitalistic bent suggested that some undefined supra-organic factor sparked those early gels. Today the more generally accepted view is that preliving systems were pushed over the fence into the field of life by the same forces of mutation and natural selection that came to be so conspicuously operative in later evolution. Mutational forces (among them, ionizing radiations, perhaps more abundant or powerful in the early days of the planet than now) could have caused certain of the gel globules, containing just the right combination of proteinlike materials, to modify or to mutate. A path of ionizing energy can alter the intimate chemical structure of a colloid particle just as easily as it can that of a gene.

Assuming the operation of mutation and selection in the environment of a prelife colloid, consider the hypothetical case of a primordial gel particle whose outer surface was selectively permeable to, say, a certain specific type of amino acid found in surrounding waters. In addition to this "food," present in the medium were two other chemicals capable in the presence of an appropriate enzyme of uniting to form more of that same needed amino acid. Suppose, then, that with the passage of time the total amount of that particular amino acid in a given environment were used up. All colloidal globules in the area chemically dependent on that amino acid would "starve" and disintegrate. The survival of any globule would be contingent on its capacity to produce minute amounts of the enzyme needed to combine the two types of other chemicals (still abundant in the medium) to form the crucial amino acid. At length, this hypothesis continues, a colloid mutant appeared which, because of its capacity to do this, survived and perpetuated this capacity in whatever globules it produced during subsequent physico-chemical divisions. Given a sufficiently long time, and presupposing the continuous action of mutating forces, other enzymatic or metabolic systems were similarly created and selected for survival, until finally certain colloids began to have so complex a biochemical pattern as to qualify them as quasi-living. They would then have come to constitute the *Urschleim* from which true protoplasm ultimately—and mysteriously, it must still be said—emerged.

Whether it happened in just this way is, of course, highly conjectural (there have been many theories to explain the origin of life, none experimentally proved). But whatever its precise details, creation viewed as a phenomenon of chemical and organic emergence is somewhat at variance with the views expressed in 1654 by the vice-chancellor of Cambridge University.

Few informed people hold any longer to the idea of a special divine creation; rather, swept along in the intellectual currents of our times, they give at least quasi acceptance to the evolutionary explanation of man's origin, of life's origin, of the planet's origin. A corollary to such belief is the hypothesis that our solar system—indeed the whole universe—is but one vast quantum of energy quivering toward an ultimate and dead equilibrium. Our sun, however, instead of initially cooling, will undergo a gradual increase in temperature, for the calculations of astrophysicists indicate that, as the sun's hydrogen component becomes consumed, the sun's nuclear fires tend to burn the more fiercely. Solar heat radiating out into space will ultimately be such as to parch the continents of our planet, then to vaporize the seas, finally, about ten billion years from now, to convert the whole orb again into a molten mass. All protoplasmic life (except, fancifully, those of the earth's inhabitants that may have migrated to some other less threatened celestial body) will perish. The sun will undergo one last death spasm of brilliant luminosity, then, cooling, will share the fate that awaits all stars—a cold, inert, energyless end.

During only one "short" period of this x-billion-year time spectrum will the surface of our planet have passed through a temperature range amenable to the chemistry of living organisms as we know them. Such a thermal range was entered on about two billion years ago; exit from it will be made a few billion years from now. There is no factual basis for assuming that the iota of time during which life has appeared and evolved on at least this one of the heavenly orbs is anything but an evanescent tick of a great cosmic clock—a clock which will stop when its spring tension has run down.

The question of how the clock came to be wound in the first place did not at the moment pose itself in the mind of that tiny spot of a man plodding there on a muddy Venezuelan plain.

By midafternoon I was standing in the shade of the Algarrobito hut. Somewhere to the southeast there must surely have been feeding shallows, but I had not reached them. The ibis formations above me had simply refused to bend earthward.

It was not this failure, however, that was causing my present dismay; it was the fate that had befallen the monk's cloth during my absence. There it lay on the grass where I had left it, but now quite unrecognizably cut into approximate 3-x-3-foot squares neatly stacked. Manuel and Ventura were obviously the culprits, but I felt that it was I who was really at fault, on account of my poor Spanish. Before setting out that morning I had tried, by means of a crude combination of manual and verbal language, to convey the idea that the monk's cloth was merely to be aired and dried, that its life of bird deception was by no means over and that it was soon to see more service in the garcero. Manuel had derived precisely the opposite impression. He seemed to have construed the previous day's demolition as evidence that the bird watching was at an end and that my throwing the cloth out on the grass was an act of final disposal.

I could easily imagine how, after I had left on my cross-country walk that morning, Manuel had sat there and contemplated the fabric, perhaps calling Ventura over for consultation. With some uncertainty the two had eased closer to examine the tempting heap. The dry season was approaching, and with it the roundup. What splendid saddle blankets this heavy coarse cloth would make! For a moment they may have hesitated; should they perhaps wait for my return and ask permission? No, the cloth had clearly been discarded. Slowly a knife was drawn from its leather waist holster. Then abruptly inhibitions and doubts vanished as the men fell to, one holding while the other applied the ripping blade.

Now in midafternoon I stood there contemplating the sorry remains, and the two men seemed uneasy as they perceived my lack of mirth. To have lost my temper would have been not only silly and pointless but wholly unfair. My linguistic limitations, already at the root of the trouble, led me to refrain from further explanatory attempts. Instead, I stooped in under the roof shelter, opened one of my bundles containing the first-aid kit and removed the largest of the curved surgical needles. Somewhere in the same bag I located a spool of heavy thread. So equipped, I sat down on the grass next to the pile of intended horse blankets, threaded my needle and began to sew. A smile thrown in the direction of the apprehensively watching Manuel and Ventura served to wash all blood from guilty hands. They broke out in happy grins and hurried over to help hold the squares as I proceeded with the big stitching job.

There would be more bird watching in the garcero, this time from a patchwork blind.

Chapter 9

TIME IS, time was, time is past. Whatever place or circumstance one associates with full emotion and pervading thought, one often comes to love. Such was the place and such the circumstance on which I was now in process of turning my back. Mists were still on the meadow that morning as my little flat-bottomed boat eased out of the grassy Matapalos channel and into the no longer fearsome Río Matillure. A pull of the starting cord and I was headed for civilization—that other world of life, growth, sex and death. I looked for the crocodile "at the gate" to receive my last waves, but he was not to be seen. Eastward was our course; our faces were tinted pink as in an underexposed Kodachrome, and the firmament was full of billowing handiwork. The motor purred faultlessly, and, before I realized it, mile after mile of jungled riverside had piled into a barrier separating me from something very dear.

I had left Algarrobito several days before, feeling reasonably satisfied that my coro-coro aims had been achieved: the scarlet ibis had been found, pictures had been taken, watching from the blind had been long, zealous and patient. Only by remaining until the garcero break-up could I have derived additional material of a natural-history value. Such a wait, however, seemed inadvisable, even futile, for not only was my equipment, one item after another, falling victim to mildew, but the waters of the garcero had already

235

started to ebb. The shutter of my camera had turned gray and on release would hesitate and wheeze, doing heaven only knew what to my exposure calculations. As to the receding waters, rain here was still a daily occurrence, but westward toward the Andes, in the upper reaches of the llanos drainage basin, the precipitation had by now passed its seasonal peak. To and from the garcero each day I had been noticing branches and leaf clusters, previously submerged, for the first time appearing above the water, muddy and silt-covered. The dirty band of foliage at the river's edge was each day becoming wider; and there was a greater frequency of our canoe getting stuck in bogs and shallows. Appearing too were purely ornithological signs of impending garcero shutdown: many an adult scarlet ibis was beginning to show a feather thinning at the neck and head, harbinger of the dry-season molt; and groups of immatures, now fully fledged, would sometimes, when disturbed, wing high into the sky, there to flash in and out of visibility as they made wide spiral revolutions, in contrast to the bush-to-bush flutterings of an earlier day.

My farewell to Algarrobito was silent and solemn, and a little sad. Manuel's and Ventura's for keeps now was the monk's cloth—godspeed the horses on whose backs it would live out the remainder of its devious life cycle. An over-the-shoulder glimpse as I rounded the river bend afforded me a final, sharp memory of Algarrobito—the incongruity of a striped orange and blue beach umbrella planted in the middle of Manuel's front yard.

And at Matapalos, too, there were ties which grew taut with sentiment only when about to be broken. But first I had rested for a few days, eaten well at Kitson's table, filled my gasoline drums and prepared for the big push back to

San Fernando. Downstream should be rapid, Kitson said; easily do it in two days. Tomás, the man Mr. Briggs had appointed to serve as my guide on the original San Fernando-Matapalos trip, was no longer around. Now at Matapalos, the only person knowing the route, other than Kitson, was old Agustin, an ancient whose skin was wrinkled and whose eyesight was not as it had once been. But he understood the vagaries of river travel and, more important, knew the great grass swamp we must cross to get from the Arauca to the Apure. Carefully Kitson prodded the old peon's memory as to where precisely we should turn north, exactly which caño would get us through. Yes, yes, Agustin understood perfectly. The evening before our departure, Kitson had sent his cook's helper out across the meadow to shoot us a lunch—a handsome wild duck which by early morning had been roasted, wrapped and, together with a loaf of bread and some fruit, put among my things. It was difficult to leave Kitson. To him went the credit for having cleared my path to the garcero; to him I would be forever indebted for unsparing hospitality, companionship and fun.

Toward evening of our first day out we encountered heavy showers. I calculated that we had done, by this time, a good fifty miles, and so had no objection to calling it a day. Sleeping in a native hut had long before lost its novelty; my earlier scruples regarding malaria, parasites and such sundry occupational hazards were gone. Indeed, I had come to look, if not entirely to feel, like a llanos peon myself. I was hardly aware of the streams of rain pouring off the straw roof as we ducked under and in, or of the little rivulets running across the hard-packed dirt floor. The woman silhouetted in the smoky glow of the cook fire under the adjoining roof, the pigs I stumbled over and sent squealing out to where the woman stood, the half-dozen nervous chickens on their perches under the eaves—these were at the heart of llanos hut life and elicited no more than a passing notice.

Agustin made our wants known to the small barefooted man in tattered shorts, and before long, having accepted tins of hot coffee and eaten of our lunch, we strung our hammocks. Watching in rapt silence were the inevitable gamin, two here, whose running noses attracted numbers of flies. The bony dogs that had yapped their lungs out at our arrival were now quietly preoccupied with very private scratchings and lickings. Darkness fell, and with it a sleep undisturbed by premonitions of the morrow.

What first produced slight doubts in my mind as to old Agustin's qualifications as a river guide were his repeated requests, during the resumed journey next morning, that I slow the boat at nearly every north-bank caño we came to. From his forward seat on the tarp-covered cargo he would search, apparently for a sign or cue of some sort, then signal me on. Twice he designated a vague foliage-hung opening as the one, finally, for which he had been on lookout, and I arced the speeding boat eagerly through it, only to be stopped within a few hundred feet by a barrier of tangled roots or bog. Both times I maneuvered a turn-about and hasty return to the Arauca for further eastbound searching. That we were now in the vicinity of the great swamp was revealed through occasional thinnings in the bank vegetation, where I could see a flatness of green extending to the horizon—a billion *Paspalum* shafts, now at the peak of their seasonal growth.

A third time, the caño Agustin designated proved to have no immediate barrier; from this one we did not return.

Almost abruptly the heaps and pillars of trees and twining lianas bordering the river and the first quarter mile of caño gave way to a pure culture of swamp grass—grass that seemed low at a distance but towering in proximity, like that encountered en route to the garcero, except that here it was even more lushly green, more fully dominating. The channel was initially about fifty feet across, tortuous and twisting, and I felt that we were entering where noise of any kind was a violation. Now on both sides vision was stopped by the virid walls of grass rising clean and sheer six to eight feet out of the flood. I recalled that when Tomás and I had passed through this same swamp earlier in the season, interior-bound, the grass was less than half its present height and could easily be seen over. I kept the outboard's throttle well advanced, for the channel was deep and free of roots or mud or floating debris. Its current was firm but not fast. Once or twice I looked back to see our wake as two giant victory fingers, causing the crags of grass to undulate precisely at our speed. Nothing broke the graveyard gloom of the swamp; there was no wind, locally no air movement, no birds feeding or flying above. Back on the broad Río Arauca our motor had hummed with a sound of life and vigor; here it was dulled as though functioning in a room hung with heavy acoustic drapery.

At this point on my map the parallel Arauca and Apure rivers were perhaps fifteen miles apart, and the problem of crossing the space between, designated on the map as *swamp* (the specific channel we followed, like all such overflow connectives of llanos rivers, was unknown to map makers), looked simple enough. In the reverse direction, I had done it in less than three hours, but that was before the grass had grown to be a forest.

After possibly an hour of travel, the green walls, I noticed, were closing in. The channel had begun to narrow, small tributaries to stray off from it; it was as if we were traveling through the outermost branches of a fallen tree. Each branch with its numerous twigs seemed identical to the next, nor did the direction of current flow retain its former constancy. Little subchannels flowed in one direction here, in another there. It seemed we were approaching the swamp's drainage divide. I had the vague feeling of being on some sort of forbidden adventure through the Land of Oz, where plants are animate and can engulf the passer-by.

At each new fork Agustin would study the two identical tines, and then, acting with reassuring directness, would indicate the one or the other for us to enter. With no basis other than a general uneasiness, I began to suspect a factor of mental coin flipping in these decisions; but no matter, for I knew that, merely by keeping the morning sun to our right, we could not fail ultimately to break out onto the Río Apure, once a feared enemy, now in the distance a beckoning friend.

The trouble was that should difficulties of an unexpected nature arise, we would find ourselves hard pressed to retrace a course to the Arauca, for by this time there had been too many branchings. We were irreversibly committed to attaining the Apure. We had no compass, but the sun's position guided us and the sky was clear.

I have said that the swamp, except for the grass itself, seemed empty of life. That we saw no water birds, other-

wise omnipresent in the llanos, struck me as peculiar, but
not after a moment's thought. In spreading high and far,
the inundating waters had tended to dilute and disperse
their own population, so as to make it an unprofitable feeding area for such birds. Had there been a garcero in the
midst of the swamp, then at least there would have been
caribes and their ecological predecessors and followers.
But this was a world of grass, lacking tree or shrub or any
other substantial support for nests.

Even had the aquatic forms been more abundant, the
channels here were presently too deep, the flats too flooded
and grass-choked for wading fishers of the heron and egret
class, and there was no exposed mud for probers of the
ibis variety. At the end of winter, llanos life tends more
and more to gather near the rivers and in such of the caños
and bayous unlikely to dry up. This is not to say that swimming under us as we passed were no fish; proof of this
would come in December, when almost suddenly the flood
waters would pour off the grass flats and rush riverward.
Wherever oxbows or ponds or pools were left, a fat concentration would occur, and fish would splash and feeders
would swarm. For a few weeks many former garcero birds
would visit the present swamp area, settling in the remnant
shallows and on soft mudbanks for a gluttonous pecking
and probing and shoveling for the millions of trapped
crustaceans, fish and worms. The very channel through
which we were moving, lifeless now, would buzz with
egrets minus their nuptial plumes, with ibises less scarlet
than before, with herons, storks and spoonbills no longer
in their winter best, but all *con mucho apetito*. When the
pools and oxbows had vanished and the mud turned into
cracked pan, the feeders would be off again, back to the

bayous near the river, where food could still be found, although not under the picnic conditions provided briefly here in the drying swamp.

But perhaps once more, later in the dry season, the feathered ones would return—this time attracted not by shrinking pools but by pillars of smoke. I had once seen it happen in the savannas of the Guiana highlands hundreds of miles to the east of here, where also during the wet season grasses grow thick and tall only to dry and die when the rains have stopped. There I saw a fire sweep across the prairie world, driving before it a terrorized population of grass and earth dwellers. The smoke coiling into the sky seemed to act as a specific signal to birds which normally cling close to the forested and watered marshes and bayous.

Here in the llanos when a grass fire breaks out, they come in clouds—the locust and grasshopper eaters, the snake and frog eaters, the mouse and shrew eaters, even the rabbit eaters—the grackles, the hawks, the egrets, the herons, the storks and all their kind. Through the skies they pour, eager to be in on the kill, for uncannily they are aware that streaming out before the spreading flame front will flee every nonsedentary inhabitant of the land, panic-stricken, leaping out of the fire into the beaks of the hungry. Stories are told of birds seen flying toward the smoke, through wisps of flame, to feed on refugees from the fire. Tiger, deer, cattle—these too will panic before the flame, but in such the birds can have no interest. After the holocaust the feeders return to their summer stations nearer water. Again the swamp is a lonely, lifeless place—a black waste now, so to remain until its sleeping seeds and roots are coaxed back to life by the first April rains.

Suddenly I slowed, then stopped the motor, for, without warning or indication, our waterway had come up against a dead end. Agustin was on his feet at once, peering through the grill of grass stalks for signs of the channel's continuance, but seeing none. For a time we drifted; clearly Agustin had made a profound miscalculation somewhere back along the line.

The sun was now high to our right, a position designating north as straight ahead. Agustin, mumbling something in Spanish, at length signaled that we resort to the obvious —in this case, reverse course. Within a quarter of a mile we came to the Y where we had made our last decision. Being fed through the grass by a diffusion of overflow water rather than by any primary stream, all three arms were of equal size, giving no clue whatever as to which, if any, was the through course or indeed which was our original. We headed into the one that seemed to bear most directly at right angles to the sun. Before long we were encountering more Ys and even Xs. By now I, at least, was completely disorientated.

Then came another dead end. Again Agustin stood up, blinking and squinting. He seemed now to be entirely at the mercy of improvisation, and I was beginning acutely to mourn his apparent lack of 20/20 vision. But suddenly and emphatically, as though he had all at once sighted some new clue, Agustin signaled for a reversal again. I spun the boat around and with a new gladness headed in the direction from which we had come. My disillusionment grew again with every yard of forward progress; only more labyrinthine branchings, none familiar, were in store for us. Each time we entered a new passageway, I would look for some characteristic of grass or channel that could be recognized in case of a forced return. But here were no blazes, no signposts. The idea occurred to me of tearing a handkerchief into ribbons and at each bifurcation tying one to a stalk—a good idea had I applied it from the beginning. Now such a system would be of no value, for we had already passed an uncounted number of openings, all indistinguishable one from the other.

An eon of time seemed to have elapsed since our entry into the swamp; by now we should have been well on the north side. I recalled the tale of the man accidentally locked in a mausoleum who, several hours later when rescue came, swore he had been there for days. I checked the gas supply —there was enough for seven hours, four of which must be saved for the Apure. The nearest fuel was at San Fernando —the journey's end—forty miles away. I tapped Agustin on the shoulder and pointed to the gas drums, to the motor, then northward, indicating the Apure. The old man seemed aware of what I was trying to communicate, and his face showed black concern. I refused to acknowledge it, smiling gaily as though being trapped in a dismal swamp were a pleasurable everyday experience for me.

There was more zigzagging, more following of possible escape routes, all of which sooner or later were sealed by walls of grass. Despite the sound of the motor and the sight of the wake behind us, I now began to have the feeling that it was we who were standing still and the grass that was moving, throwing up walls before us, dissolving them, rebuilding them elsewhere. At one point I turned off the motor and, for the purpose of conserving gas, suggested an interlude of poling, but for this the water proved too deep. Then I decided to cover a lot of territory rapidly, on the theory that the more paths probed, the more likely, statistically, would be our chance of outmaneuvering the trap. Starting the motor and giving her full throttle, I speeded the boat, almost recklessly, out of one capillary into another, out of that one and into the next. Ashamed of myself for this premature show of panic, I soon thought better of so profligate a use of precious fuel. Also I was recalling the ease with which at the garcero Manuel and Ventura and I had solved the difficulty of a similar maze. On the other hand, I was very much aware of the danger of trying to negotiate grass in a flat-bottomed boat, especially for one completely unfamiliar with the terrain and accompanied by an ancient of failing eyesight and perhaps limited endurance.

There was no rule that I knew of regarding the distribution or configuration of water channels; some parts of a llanos swamp may be a virtual *rete mirabile;* others, solid unbroken grass. I had heard stories of canoes found lying high and dry on a summertime plain. A few yards away would be the canoeist's bones, telling the tale of that final frantic prestarvation attempt to break through the imprisoning grass on foot. Of caribes or caimans or tigers one need have little fear here—only exhaustion and starvation or, if one left the boat, ultimate drowning. The lunch prepared for us at Matapalos was at this point reduced to half a loaf of bread and a few chewed-on sinews of wild duck. Agustin had some pieces of crust tied in his bundle. We had planned to reach San Fernando within two days and had brought no excess provender. For fresh water we were limited to the volume of a swamp fifteen miles across. We were certainly nowhere near starvation or even the early stages of debility, but our prospects, based on the total picture, were discomfiting.

Whether we perished afloat in an exitless maze of water or wedged in deep grass did not appear to make much difference; so at the next northern dead end I speared the boat into the green wall, cut the motor, lifted the prop and ducked my head as we came in contact with the true enemy. Here we found the water to be only three or four feet deep; so Agustin, changing seats with me so as to be in the stern, immediately went to work with his pole, while I tugged on handfuls of the surrounding stalks. After only a few minutes of this the boat was clothed, all except the stern, in a strait jacket of green. Instead of separating the grass as a dugout does, our boat flattened it out and rode over. The underlay of prone stalks was fresh glue, and we advanced only a foot or so with each thrust of the pole and tug on the grass. Behind us the overrun grass lay prostrate, leaving a track which, happily, we would be able to follow in case reversal was ultimately called for. Then I was disturbed by the sight, about fifty feet back, of the grass shafts rising slowly, like animated bowling pins, to resume their original erect positions.

At the very moment of that melancholy observation the bow broke into open water and we were floating free in another channel. I gave myself no time to feel elated, instead quickly lowered the prop and started the motor. This waterway led northeastwardly, and in that direction I set out at full speed. For a few minutes I breathed with composure, thinking wishfully that the crisis was over, but only until another green barrier loomed up. It seemed to reach the sky.

In view of the previous good luck, as well as my reborn anxiety, I did not hesitate to run the boat directly into the wall. With great and desperate energy now we resumed the process of poling and tugging. Again I looked back and saw the grass we had run over slowly rising. But we kept on, making sure by the sun that our course was ever northward. Even if it took days, this sort of progress should eventually get us through.

Imperceptibly we were entering an area where the grass was even thicker and denser than before. It hung like witch fingers around us. It brushed my face with the caresses of a sadist, scraped my neck with the tenderness of a thousand untied nooses. The mat under the boat had the sticking properties of mire, which seemed to become ever more viscous. Agustin and I were panting, mainly for physiological reasons, but I could sense the development of psychological undertones. Finally in despair I called a halt. We must turn back before our path was altogether obliterated by the rising stalks.

When we again achieved open water, I had the feeling of a prisoner who, having tunneled out of his cell, comes up only to find himself in the middle of the prison yard— free from immediate bars but still surrounded by penitentiary walls. Sometime earlier I had tried to get Agustin to lift me on his shoulders so as to get a full view over these walls but had not been able to attain the required elevation.

While sitting there trying to recover my breath and feeling not nearly so grateful as I should have for at least being out of the cell, I put the matter bluntly up to Agustin. How serious was this situation? His excited replies, as much as I understood of them, seemed to indicate that natives occasionally canoe through this swamp as a short cut between the Arauca and the Apure, but that such traffic is never heavy, a fact to which, on the basis of five hours of present experience, I could easily attest. If we had not wandered too far off course . . . But the look on Agustin's face revealed a fear that we might have done just that. Previously I had been uneasy; now I was alarmed. As a first emergency measure I decided that there would be no more of this burying ourselves in deep grass, where we could not see or be seen and where, in addition, we were always risking the gravest of ends—getting inextricably stuck. We must at all costs now find a place where the grass could somehow be seen over, and there we must maintain a continuous lookout. If by tomorrow no one came within sight or signal, I would tie a white shirt to the pole and hoist it above the grass, or possibly build a smoke fire on the surface of one of the empty gas drums.

I started the motor and edged along slowly. A mild breeze had arisen which laid the grass a good head lower than before—which was a huge break for us. We came to a trough in the grass sea where, by standing high, I could command a view; this would be our waiting station. Far, far to the north I could see the bank jungle of the Río Apure as a pale-purple line; far, far to the south, another such line. Each must have been a good six or seven miles away, for we were at almost dead center of the swamp. The intervening spaces lacked even a mirage for encouragement; nor was there any evidence of the great sheet of water which lay under the grass or of the myriad channels wriggling through it.

I do not know why I started at this point to shout, for clearly there was no one around to hear me. If I expected heads of eager rescuers to pop up all around, I must have been out of my mind; there was no sign of life anywhere. I yelled first in one direction, then in another. My voice seemed to be absorbed and deadened before it got even beyond my teeth. Agustin stood and, cupping his hands, began to shout too, making it a peculiar duet. The timbre of his aged vocal cords sounded like a ghostly echo of my own.

I could not avoid an occasional worried reflection on what would happen if no help came by tomorrow or the next day or the next. In desperation we would, of course, be driven eventually to set out again, probing the open water in all directions, then at last lured again into the grass. There, unless by the grace of a merciful heaven we could intercept a through channel, we would finally be stopped by sheer exhaustion—caught and held fast, out of sight of all but the vultures who would sooner or later appear overhead. I dared for a moment to contemplate the mechanics of death here in a grass-shrouded tomb—the nights, the mosquitoes, the growing debility, the sun- and rain-drenched period of senselessness, perhaps the ravings, and then the final curtain. Agustin, being an old man, would probably go first, and I would spend my last hours, perhaps days, in the congenial company of a corpse. Such thoughts caused the tissues of my mouth to dry. I picked up the canteen of chlorozoned water. But bacteria, pathogenic or harmless, seemed very unimportant at this juncture of my career. I recalled those nicely conceived ideas on the origin, evolution and fate of the planet's first single-celled microbes. Then I threw down the canteen and leaned over the side of the boat and cupped handfuls of cooler swamp water to my mouth.

I was no longer a biologist studying or contemplating life from a distance. I was now myself one of those survive-if-you-can creatures. I thought of the pits of La Brea, in geologically recent times consisting of soft tar overlaid by pools of rain water. Hoofed animals, wading into the shallows to drink, would get caught. Their dying screams would attract flesh eaters—saber-tooth tigers, wolves, vultures. These too, unwary of the tar's softness, would find themselves stuck while trying to devour those already trapped. Like quicksand, the tar would draw the strugglers down for embalmment, there to await the excavating paleontologist. I had been attracted to the green "tar pits" of this grassy land not by any screams of the scarlet ibis but by its color. Wolves would not come, nor saber-tooth tigers, but vultures. . . .

Men frequently build their fears far in excess of those justified by the real hazard: under anxiety, telegrams become death notices, late trains become wrecks, upset stomachs become cancer. To avoid such excesses, I made an effort to take stock of the present situation analytically. I had been in tight spots before and had always managed somehow to come through. I did not carry a rabbit's foot, but to date I had a good survival record. Here I was, reasonably young and healthy, with at the very least three days to go before any sort of disabling debility would set in. Captain Bligh and his men had stayed alive 41 days in an open boat, and they were surrounded by brine, not fresh potable water. I chided myself for imagining so prematurely that by moving northward, even through a glue of heavy grass, we could not succeed eventually in breaking through the five or so miles that separated us from the Apure. To prove the point, I did a little mental arithmetic: in one hour we had done perhaps 300 feet through the grass. If we worked twelve continuous hours a day, that would in three days be about 10,800 feet, somewhat over two miles! Well, then, how about canoe traffic through the swamp? I might have been optimistic about this had it not been for Agustin's statement that such traffic, never heavy, is wholly unpredictable and that we might not be aware of it even if it were near. By reaching up to full height I could see over the grass now. But a native poling or paddling a dugout would more than likely be too low to see or be seen. Then I tried to dispel my fears by the use of statistics: in the mortality tables, probably not more than one person in a billion expires lost in a swamp. This would make my survival chance here far better than in a train, airplane or car; and certainly when traveling by any of these means I did not each time go into a state of trembling anxiety.

But try as I might, I could not wish away my apprehensions. Statistics are group matters and cannot be used to predict individual cases. Moreover, I knew that no one was expecting us in San Fernando, and there was neither radio nor telephone connection that would enable Kitson to check on our arrival. We would not be missed for months. A flyer downed at sea in a raft knows that the combined Navy, Coast Guard and Air Force are combing the area for him.

The more I tried to buoy myself, the more apparent it became that this was no mere play on my suggestibility. To a man under capital sentence, death is as real, probably even more real, weeks before he walks to the chair than a few moments before the current is turned on. Despite the fact that we had actually been lost now for only five hours, the image of our condition three or four days hence had a devastating impact. The very idea of languishing here, stuck in a grave of grass and water, started the gamut of physiological stress reactions: glands were ready to pour out emergency hormones, neural centers to choke up with conflicting impulses, internal biochemistry to release additional energy. All these reactions, designed by the body's architects to sharpen the animal for combat or flight, would be frustratingly without point or purpose here. I shook my head and stood up for more peering and calling to the horizon. But my shouts were answered only by the rustle of gently tossing grass tops.

Agustin did not show signs of the sort of fear that was welling up in me, and yet I knew from the emotional quality of his earlier shouts that he fully shared my cognizance of what we were facing. Perhaps he was too old to feel life's clinging ties as strongly as I; perhaps he was a wise man. I was remembering a quotation from the past: "The wise man fears not death, before which most men tremble." Agustin sat with bowed head, much as if in prayer.

I myself had long ignored personal religion as a crutch I did not need, organized religion as ancient mysticism superimposed on expedient morality. I had generally gone along with the view that man is a psychological reactor system, differing from the chimpanzee mainly in the possession of better calculating equipment and a greater capacity for subjectivity and self-awareness. The latter factor I had regarded as synonymous with the classical but now fairly defunct idea of "soul." Thus I believed that when the body dies and the mind necessarily ceases to function, the "soul" too must vanish—like the image on a screen when the projector light is turned off. Before the laws of nature and the cosmos, to a universal energy—before these I would humble myself, but before no personalized God. My creed was to accept what came within the power of my limited sensory and mental equipment to grasp, and no more—which in this case would be a through channel to the Apure or the appearance of a rescuing canoe.

But any solitary contemplation, especially when coupled with anxiety or suffering, seems as though by pattern almost inevitably to turn to or draw sustenance from some degree of mysticism. I was looking skyward now; my eyes were on a white cloud, then they were piercing through it into the blue beyond. I certainly had no expectation of seeing a piece of heaven there, or some great beckoning Hand; I had no hope of hearing a Voice. All I saw was space going on and on—interplanetary space to interstellar space to infinity. My consciousness was simultaneously extending in the opposite direction, down through the mud of the swamp, 8,000 miles through the earth, again into space, and again into infinity. Neither mathematically nor sensorially had I ever been able to come near to appreciating infinity; perhaps it was this deficiency that caused me now to feel the tempting tug, the solacing touch of mysticism, as I dwelt on my relation, as a threatened highly finite organism, to an incomprehensible infinity where space and time fuse.

That this was a reaction not uncommon to those in real or imagined danger I was well aware. I recalled images of the martyr at the stake proclaiming that he sees the pearly gates ajar, of the drowning man viewing a recap of his whole life as in a speeded-up movie, or of the man dying in his bed amid visions of impending glory. I was reminded that fasting, flagellation, deprivation, self-torture in a hundred different forms have all been practiced by the traditional mystic in an effort to force a rapport between mundane consciousness and some supramundane awareness not ordinarily achieved in the course of normal living. Surely a certain airiness growing now out of my anxiety was nothing more than a coloring induced by the biochemistry of stress combined with a wishful escape euphoria. The Bernadette sort of manifestation I had, more or less in vogue with modern psychiatric thinking, always regarded as paranoid. The conversion of St. Paul, even the agonies of Christ, as well as a thousand other classical cases of religious experience, I had dismissed glibly, in the manner of many of my fellows, as varieties of the paranoid syndrome.

In view of this I was somewhat confounded to find myself arguing now in the silence of a llanos swamp that to give such phenomena a modernized name is neither to clarify nor to explain them. With fancied logic and persuasiveness I asked myself: why do the mountain ranges of history tower with the peaks of men projecting their hopes above the world of matter, breaking out of the limitations of mind and senses? Must one categorically be mad or fear-ridden to penetrate beyond the limits of sensory perception? Or is religious revelation possibly quite the opposite of madness—a profound break-through to reality?

Again drifting through my mind was a recollection of those recent days when, sitting in the garcero blind or walking across muddy fields, I had pondered various biological characteristics of my surroundings. Here lost and facing an uncertain future, I found myself bumptiously challenging the whole principle of objectivity. One after another I marshaled up arguments attacking the intellectual versus the mystical approach to phenomena. Actually —I preached to myself—what the hard-boiled realist calls reality is possibly made unreal by the very nature of his analytical objectivity, for the object abstracted out of context has, as philosophers have long been saying, little meaning. That is why art and classical science are antithetical: art attempts to reassemble fragments into one meaningful whole, classical science to break the whole into fragments. Many a man has reached the conclusion that the mind cannot possibly view phenomena truthfully because the processes by which man thinks are in themselves part of the thing being thought about—"a hunter of shadows, himself a shade." For this reason any idea must of necessity reflect the morphology and the state of mind in which the idea arises. We shape our gods and our devils in our own image, as we do also the psychological designations that have come to replace the more ancient and now more or less discarded deities.

I was amused suddenly to find that this little boat had become my pulpit, the swamp my cathedral, the grass stalks my congregation—amused and a little taken aback. No prophet, I was at least the voice of one crying in a wilderness. Hastily I set aside my critique of pure reason.

I turned to Agustin. Earlier I had seen him make the sign of the cross; now it seemed that he too was engaged in his own quiet philosophizing. I could guess that the thoughts passing through his mind were of a more stereotyped nature than mine, based on a series of simple, clearly defined conceptions of life, death and the hereafter. Agustin's philosophizing consisted not of analytics but of fervent prayer to precise images of God, Christ and the Virgin—the personifications of his faith and hope.

The words *faith* and *hope* would not leave me. Were they—faith and hope—the psychological devices whereby the wise man achieves his disdain for death? That these are the two human qualities which psychology and psychiatry have not been able to reach seemed odd, as I ruminated on.

The expression "projected desires" impressed me as so much tautology, and meaningful only if some basis can be assigned for the projected desiring. Religion, I recognized now, has proverbially assayed to do this; whole creeds have been based on the simple notions of faith and hope as connectives between this world and a possible other. The third classical virtue did not much enter my thoughts, for charity is the social virtue, concerning one's relations with others, not primarily one's relations with oneself. Faith and hope, on the other hand—these are the most personal and mystical of all man's subjective qualities.

If by faith and hope the wise man escapes his fear of death, in what is he having faith and hope? I waited for my congregation of grass stalks to chant back: "In God, the Father Almighty, Maker of Heaven and earth, and in . . ." But the stalks remained mute, some nodding, some tossing their heads, as though of split opinion.

Every man, wise or foolish, knows that ultimately he cannot escape the grim reaper and that sooner or later his body must fall and return to the dust from whence it came. Does perhaps the wise man differ from the foolish in the possession of a hope, stated or implied, that death is not the end? And is it perhaps not this hope that dispels his natural fear of death? The word *soul*, used to denote a surviving entity, has long been dropped from the vocabulary of psychology; and even many of the conventional religions use the word these days only mincingly to describe a quality that at death ceases to be or reverts pantheistically back to the great impersonal kettle. Few these days, other than the most extreme fundamentalists, consider the soul to be a discrete factor which at death leaves the body and thereafter carries on a conscious higher-plane existence. The modern trend has moved us so completely to accept demonstrability as a pre-eminent value, social justice as its own end, physical health and well-being as the most valuable of one's possessions, that today for a person to harbor the idea that spiritual existence, in its true religious sense, is something apart and separate—to believe this today is a sign of intellectual immaturity, or that one is in the clutches of a dogma or is the victim of a recrudescent childhood fantasy. No wonder most men quake before the thought of death; no wonder, indeed, that mankind seems to be more uneasy than in the days of orthodoxy. Man—and, alas, I— have come to have faith and hope only in the tangible, only in the sensorially demonstrable, where those values are patently superfluous. The methods of modern science, incredibly impressive to be sure in the world of sensory experience, have become our Golden Calf; the precepts of psychology and psychiatry are becoming a widely accepted substitution for religious, mystic and poetic transcendentalism.

It struck me that what distinguishes man from the other animals is not so much the greater capacity of his intellect but his enormously greater potential for hope. A root growing toward water it cannot see, or a salmon swimming upriver to an unknown spawning site, or a caribou migrating across the range to valleys previously unvisited—none of these actions is sparked by hope or faith; they are instinctual reactions to genic or physiological stimuli. Nor does the embryo grow in any sort of faith that in so doing it will attain the state of adulthood, or the flower in blooming that it will attract insects to fertilize its ova. Man, to be sure, in view of his evolutionary past, is heavily motivated and actuated by instinct also, but only through his faith and hope qualities does he differ—except, obviously, in mental degree—from the creatures of patterned behavior; only thus does he bear witness to a Greatness beyond the senses. The wise man fears not death because he has a projected confidence in the future. For an Agustin or a Socrates, for a believer or a philosopher, hope is the essence on which life feeds, the essence before which death flees.

It occurred to me that no man is truly without hope. The suicide, the misanthrope, the melancholic—these have not lost hope. Theirs has merely been overlaid by a neuro- or psychopathic involvement, hiding their hope as sand hides a coin lost on the beach. Scrape away the sand and you find the coin; remove the involvement and you find hope again. This is at the heart of all religious conversion, from St. Paul to Billy Graham; the heart of all psychotherapy, from Christ to Menninger.

There, lost in the swamp, Agustin and I stood staring out over the grass, one of us a believer in the precepts of a formalized religion, the other ostensibly a free thinker. Yet each of us was being sustained at this very moment by the hope that nothing can really end.

The sun was falling low in the west, and the great orange-and-pink cloud masses could appropriately have been the stained-glass windows of a Gothic church. Suddenly my eyes resolved the outline of a human head not more than two hundred yards away, resting on—no, moving across—the grass. I may previously have suspected myself of dementia; now that suspicion was confirmed as fact. I think I even started to sit down and rest, to allow the macabre illusion to dissolve. The knowledge that I had become a victim of hallucinations swept over me as a disappointment, for this was surely an indication that my previous high thoughts, inklings rather, would also fall into the category of psychological aberrancy. But when I straightened up for another look the head was still there, and I could make out what looked like a poling stick moving up and down in the slow cadence of a canoeist.

"Agustin," I cried, "there!" When the old man saw the vision—the vision of a reality we had been hoping all afternoon to see—I could hear him beginning hoarsely and unbelievingly to call out. I shouted too and waved wildly with a handkerchief. Movement stopped; the head turned and looked our way. It appeared to be watching us, then started to move again. Quietly, frozen now and above further shouting, we watched the apparition, half silhouette, half rosy in the evening sun. First it moved southward for a while across the grass, then east, then west, then south again—following a channel unseen by us, just as a real canoeist would have done.

It both chilled and thrilled me to see that the head was coming closer. Finally when it was no more than a hundred feet off it stopped, and Agustin yelled something. For Agustin rather than me to call out seemed sensible, for ghosts in these parts would be familiar with Spanish rather than with English. "Please, friend," Agustin was saying in effect, "please help us. Where is the channel to the Apure?" Just then the image disappeared, and I knew that Agustin and I had indeed turned into madmen. I gulped and was about to sit down and wait for the cloak of night when the head reappeared, as is the custom in dreams—a head served up to us on a platter of green.

Only when I heard a voice barely penetrating the distance across the grass speaking in the tongue of the land, did I begin seriously to question the head's illusory character. I did not understand what the voice said, but I comprehended it fully. Into the grass in the direction of the head our boat automatically started, with Agustin poling and me tugging, like two men working their way back from the brink of Niagara. The rate at which we plowed through that grass was as miraculous as the visitation itself.

We broke into the open capillary to find that the head belonged to a simple peon, on his way home to the Arauca after a few days' visit with some relatives on the Apure. I noticed that he was tall as llanos peons go. He seemed a little surprised to see us, but mostly at the odd shape of our boat. Agustin and I were not yet in complete control of our faculties; the peon thought this was due to an exhaustion caused by the hundred-foot sprint through the impenetrable grass. He gave no indication of sensing that we had been on the verge of resigning ourselves to a fate no worse than death.

He was now carrying on a quiet conversation with Agustin, pointing northward and zigzagging his hand to indicate a route out of the capillary maze to the main channel. By this time he may have seen that we were so suspicious and fearful of the swamp that we dared not set out alone. In any case, he offered to escort us to a point from where there could be no chance of our getting lost again. His pole was about twice the length of ours; with each stroke it seemed to dip into the water about six feet. I started our motor, and its sound was that of abbey choirs. We followed closely behind the poling savior. Finally after about a half hour of familiar zigzagging, I saw that the capillaries were getting broader, the currents more consistent. We at length came to one where the current was actually swift, flowing directly north. Here the man stopped; this stream would take us to the Apure. There was a little more palavering with Agustin, and then our rescuer turned south as we entered the current and I threw the throttle open full speed. A minute or two later, when I looked back, the polesman had disappeared—I think beyond the high grass.

On the chance that the reader may wish to probe more deeply into some of the technical and speculative matters alluded to in the foregoing pages, the following works are cited as ones that the writer has found particularly stimulating.

Armstrong, E. A. *Bird display and behavior*. New York, Oxford University Press, 1947.

Bates, Marston. *Where winter never comes*. New York, Charles Scribner's Sons, 1952.

Beach, F. A. *Hormones and behavior*. New York, Paul A. Hoeber, 1948.

Beebe, William. *High jungle*. New York, Duell, Sloan & Pearce, 1949.

Berrill, N. J. *Sex and the nature of things*. New York, Dodd, Mead & Co., 1953.

Blum, H. F. *Time's arrow in evolution*. Princeton, N. J., Princeton University Press, 1951.

Bourlière, François. *The natural history of mammals*. New York, Alfred A. Knopf, 1954.

Burnet, F. M. *Biological aspects of infectious disease*. New York, The Macmillan Co., 1940.

Caullery, Maurice. *Parasitism and symbiosis*. London, Sidgwick and Jackson, Ltd., 1952.

Cherrie, G. K. *Dark trails*. New York, G. P. Putnam's Sons, 1930.

Crist, R. "Life in the llanos of Venezuela." Bulletin of the Geographic Society of Philadelphia, Vol. 35, 1937.

Cutright, P. R. *The naturalists explore South America*. New York, The Macmillan Co., 1940.

Ditmars, R. L. *Reptiles of the world*. New York, The Macmillan Co., 1933.

Dobzhansky, T. "Evolution in the tropics." *American Scientist*, Vol. 38, 1950.

Dunn, L. C. (Ed.) *Genetics in the 20th century.* New York, The Macmillan Co., 1951.

Fox, D. L. *Animal biochromes and structural colours.* New York, Cambridge University Press, 1953.

Fritsch, F. E. *The structure and reproduction of the algae.* Vol. 1. New York, Cambridge University Press, 1935.

Gamow, G. *Biography of the earth.* New York, the Viking Press, 1943.

———. *The birth and death of the sun.* New York, Penguin Books, Inc., 1945.

Hesse, R., Allee, W. C., and Schmidt, K. P. *Ecological animal geography.* New York, John Wiley and Sons, Inc., 1951.

Huxley, Julian. *Evolution, the modern synthesis.* New York, Harper & Bros., 1943.

Jepson, G. L., Simpson, G. G., Mayr, E. (Eds.) *Genetics, Paleontology, and Evolution.* Princeton, N. J., Princeton University Press, 1949.

Jurji, E. J. (Ed.) *The great religions of the modern world.* Princeton, N. J., Princeton University Press, 1947.

Kendeigh, S. C. *Parental care and its evolution in birds.* Urbana, Illinois, University of Illinois Press, 1952.

Krutch, J. W. *The measure of man.* Indianapolis, The Bobbs-Merrill Co., 1954.

Loeb, Leo. *The biological basis of individuality.* Springfield, Illinois, Charles C. Thomas, 1945.

Miller, S. L. "A production of amino acids under possible primitive earth conditions." *Science,* Vol. 117, p. 528, 1953.

Oberling, Charles. *The riddle of cancer.* New Haven, Yale University Press, 1944.

Oparin, A. I. *The origin of life.* New York, The Macmillan Co., 1938.

Penard, T. E. Section on "Scarlet Ibis," pages 33-45, in A. C. Bent's *Life histories of North American marsh birds.* Bulletin 135, Smithsonian Institution, Washington, 1926.

Redfield, Robert (Ed.) *Levels of integration in biological and social systems.* Lancaster, Pa., The Jaques Cattell Press, 1942.

Richards, P. W. *The tropical rain forest.* New York, Cambridge University Press, 1952.

Romer, A. S. *Man and the vertebrates.* Chicago, University of Chicago Press, 1941.

————. *Vertebrate paleontology.* Chicago, University of Chicago Press, 1953.

Schrödinger, Erwin. *What is life?* New York, The Macmillan Co., 1945.

Scott, W. B. *A history of land mammals in the western hemisphere.* New York, The Macmillan Co., 1937.

Simpson, G. G. *The meaning of evolution.* New Haven, Yale University Press, 1952.

Tinbergen, N. *Social behavior in animals.* New York, John Wiley & Sons, 1953.

Thompson, D. W. *Growth and form.* New York, The Macmillan Co., 1948.

Von Hagen, V. W. *South America called them; explorations of the great naturalists.* New York, Alfred A. Knopf, 1945.

Young, J. Z. *The life of vertebrates.* New York, Oxford University Press, 1952.